CONTEMPORARY GUITAR PICKING TECHNIQUE

25 SOLOS TO DEVELOP PICKING FLUENCY

KEIJO PENNANEN

Online Audio

To access the online audio recording go to:
WWW.MELBAY.COM/31064MEB

I0805684

Preface

This book presents 25 original guitar solo compositions written to promote versatile plectrum playing while also using hybrid and fingerstyle techniques. By learning and practicing these tunes, guitarists can develop the use of all three techniques in their playing. Each picking technique has its advantages, and this element has been considered in creating these settings.

Flatpicking engenders clear and even tone and dynamic changes, whereas in hybrid picking, plectrum and fingers cross the strings making it more suitable for some chord voicings and arrangements that skip strings. Although the focus of this book is on plectrum playing, fingerstyle is incorporated in pieces that benefit from a slightly softer sound.

Changing from plectrum to fingerstyle playing within the same piece can be challenging, but guitarists usually find their own way of making the switch without missing a beat. Personally, I keep the plectrum inside my hooked index (*i*) finger and use the thumb (*p*) and three remaining fingers (*m*, *a*, *c* or pinky) for picking. Others manage to "palm" or lightly grip the pick in the center of their palm, freeing up all righthand fingers for picking. Both approaches allow players to keep the pick "close at hand" at all times. I recommend that you experiment to find the best way to hold the temporarily unused pick.

The book is written in standard notation with suggested chord symbols and left and righthand fingerings. A key to the fingering indications used here can be found on page 4. Note that the fingerings offer options for the player, especially for the right hand.

In addition to its sheet music, the book includes access to online audio recordings of all 25 solos.

I sincerely hope you enjoy the compositions in this book!

Keijo Pennanen

Contents

Title	Page	Audio
Preface	2	
About the Fingering Markings	4	
Lament in E Minor	5	1
Nordic Road	6	2
Bring the Celebration	8	3
Autumn Soliloquy	10	4
Spring Views	12	5
Dedication	14	6
Navigator	16	7
Chordinator	18	8
On the Move	20	9
Family Tree	22	10
The Old Neighborhood	24	11
The Old Neighborhood Solo Chorus	26	12
Forest Play	28	13
Island Tones	30	14
Stairway of Time	32	15
Outbound Shuffle	34	16
Notes of Winter	36	17
Beantown Funk	38	18
Toward Home	42	19
Samba Shoreline	44	20
Portrait of a Memory	48	21
Cielo Nocturno	50	22
Twelfth Moment	52	23
A New Frontier	54	24
Un Poco de Flamenco	57	25
About the Author	60	

About the Fingering Markings

⑥ Circled numbers indicate the string where a note is played.

1 Plain numbers suggest left-hand fingering.

⊓ Downstroke with the pick.

V Upstroke with the pick.

CII The letter C and accompanying Roman numeral indicate a barré and the fret position.

Right-hand fingering symbols are derived from the Spanish names for the fingers:

p A note played by the right-hand thumb or *pulgar*.

i Index finger—*indice*

m Middle finger—*medio*

a Ring finger—*anular*

c little finger—*chico*; sometimes *e*, *ñ* or *q* from *meñique* or *pequeño*, or *e* or *x* from *extremo*.

T Tapping.

X String muting with the fretting hand.

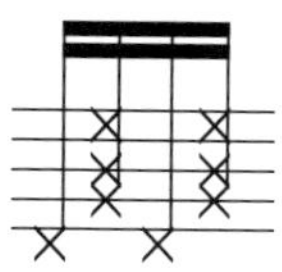

Lament in E Minor

Largo (♩ = ca. 56)

Keijo Pennanen

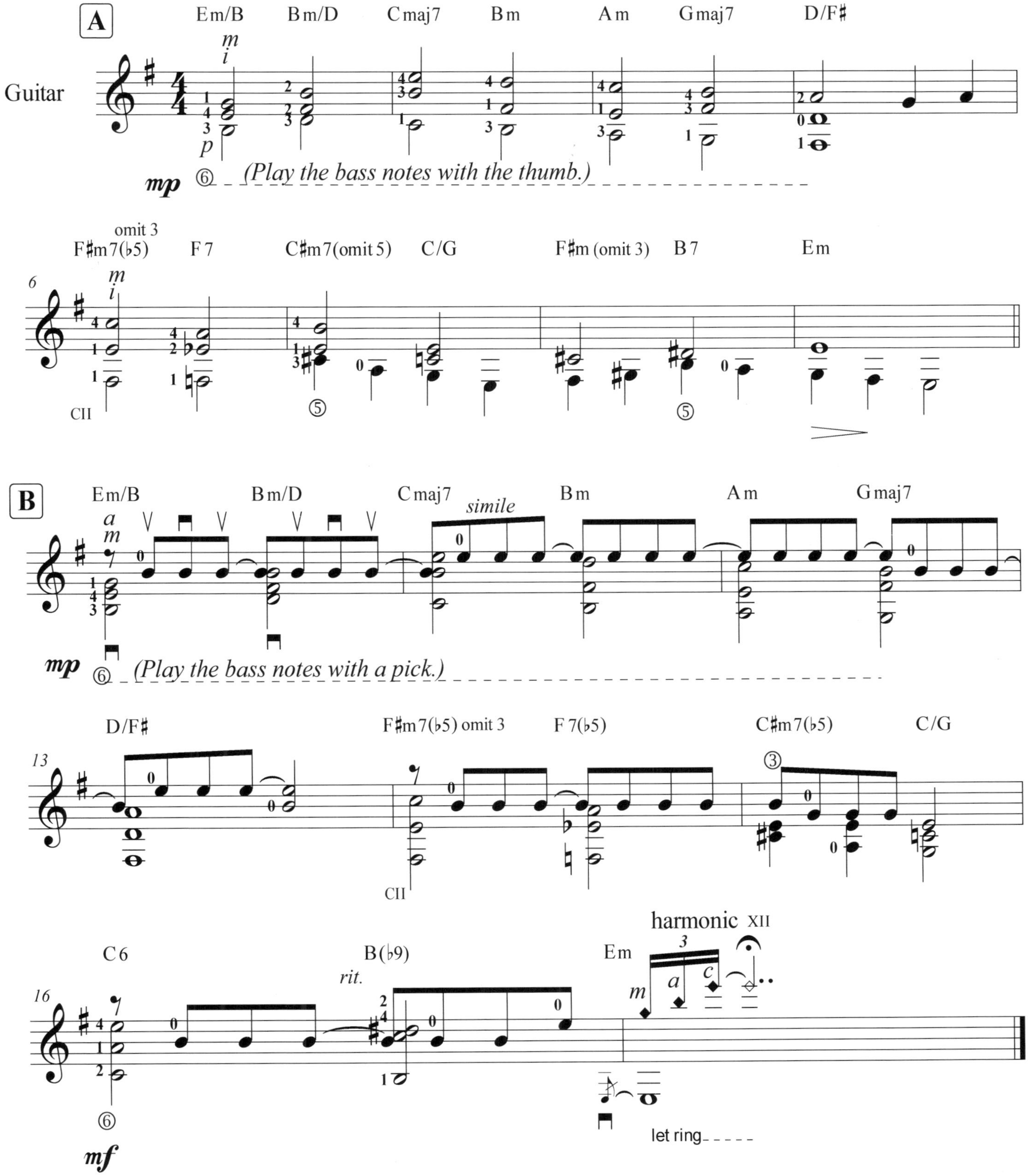

Nordic Road

Andante (♩ = ca. 90)

Keijo Pennanen

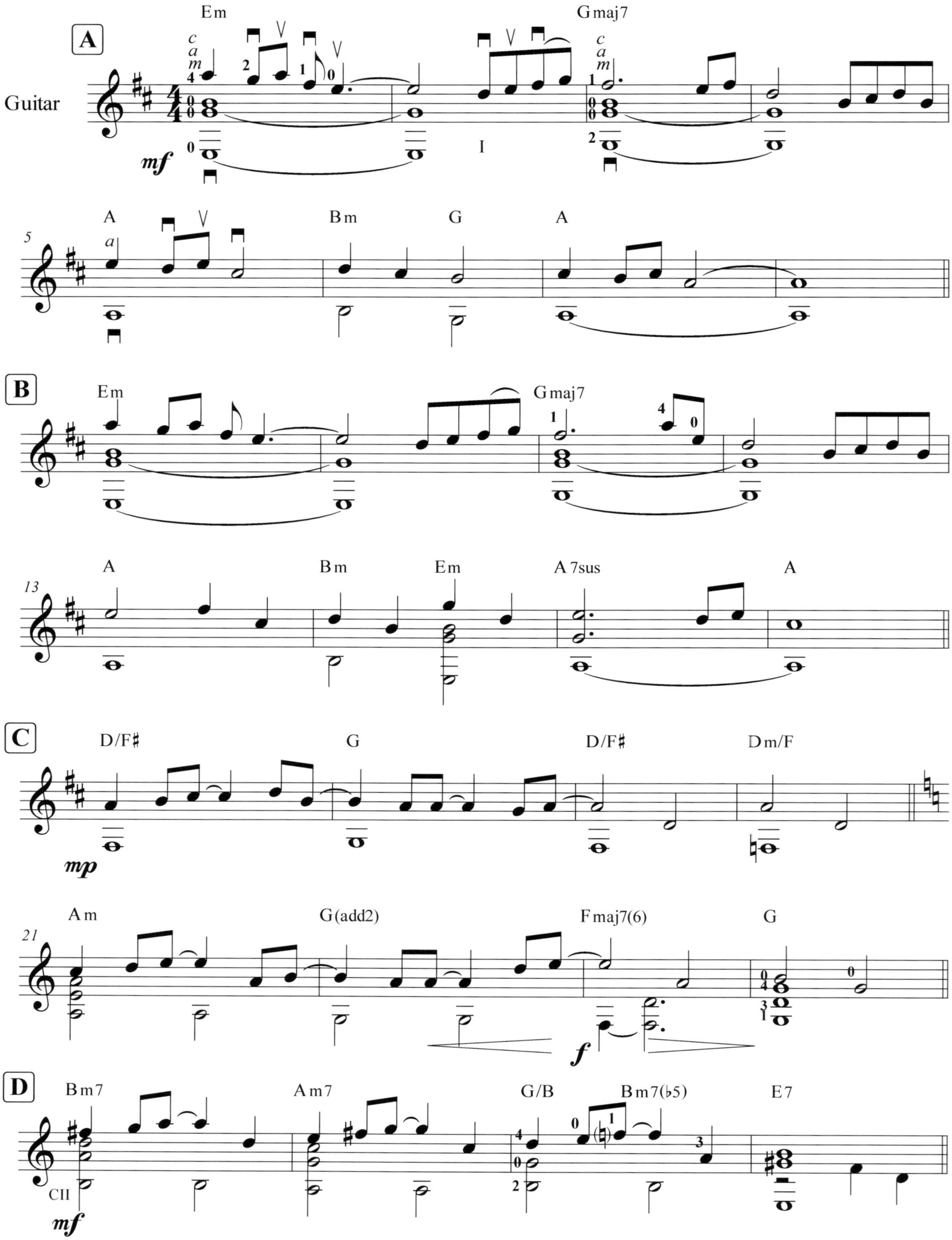

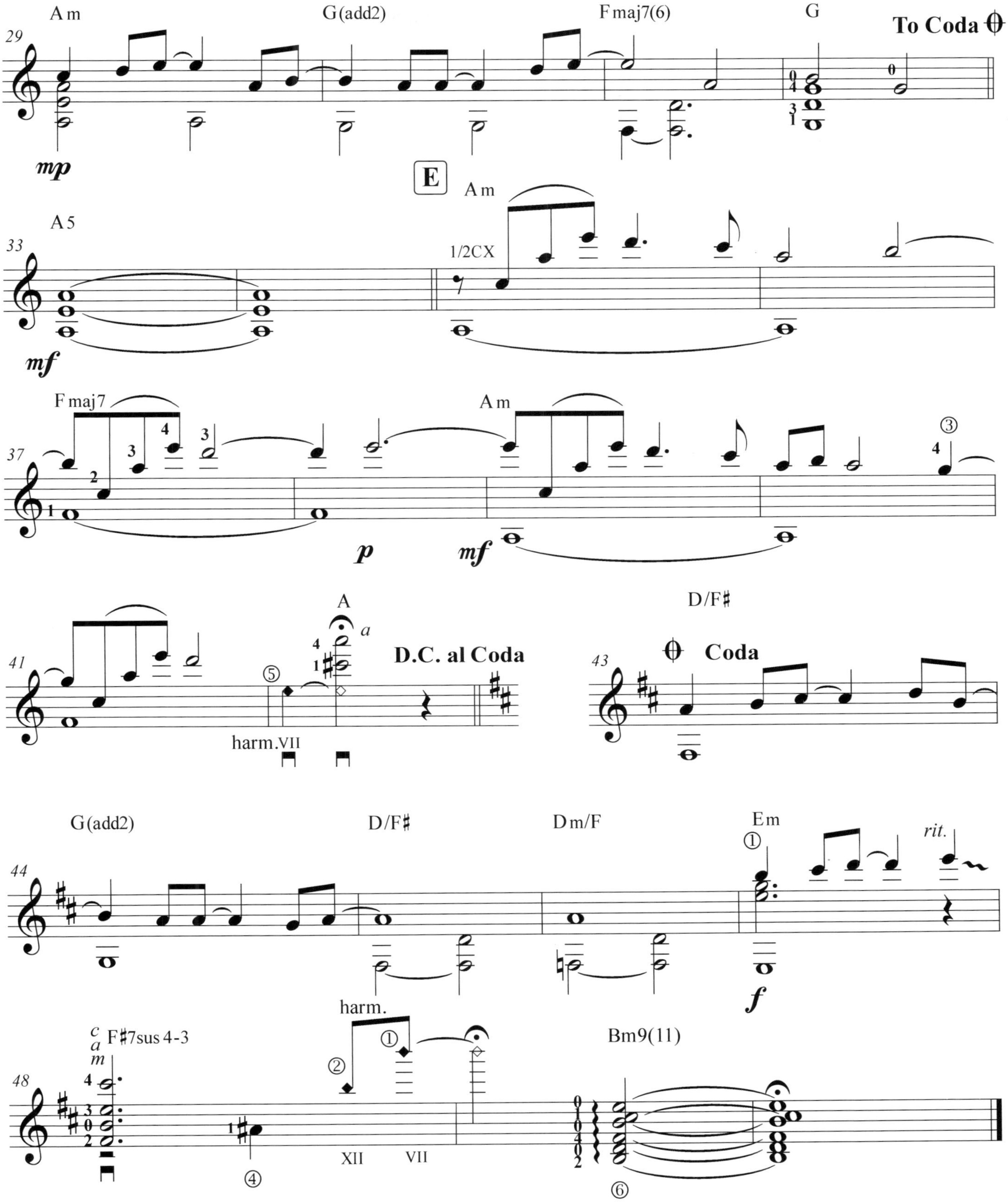
Am
G(add2)
Fmaj7(6)
G
To Coda
mp
E
A5
Am
1/2CX
mf
Fmaj7
Am
p
mf
A
a
D.C. al Coda
harm.VII
D/F♯
Coda
G(add2)
D/F♯
Dm/F
Em
rit.
f
c
a
m
F♯7sus 4-3
harm.
XII
VII
Bm9(11)

Bring the Celebration

Adagio (♩ = ca. 68) **Maestoso**

Keijo Pennanen

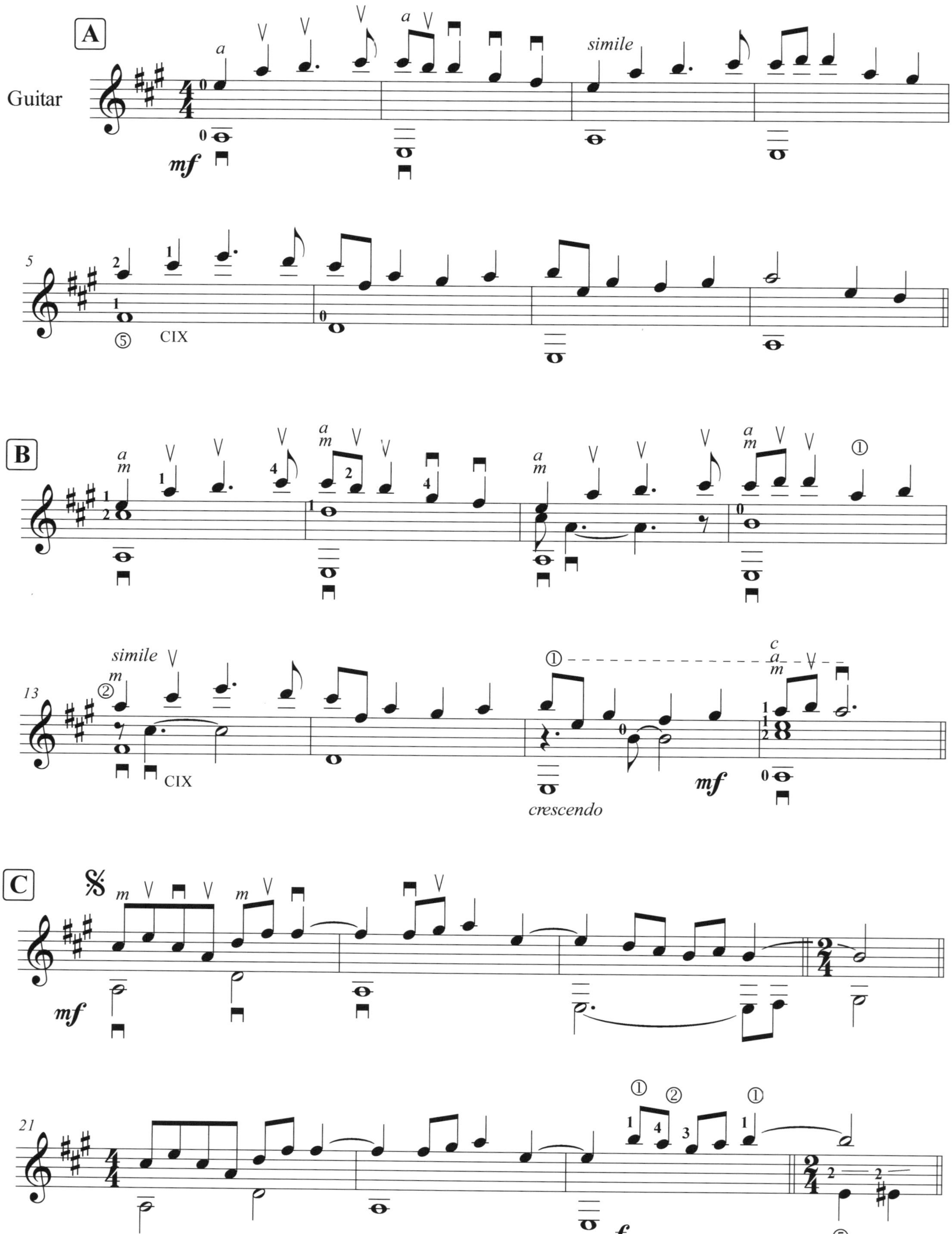

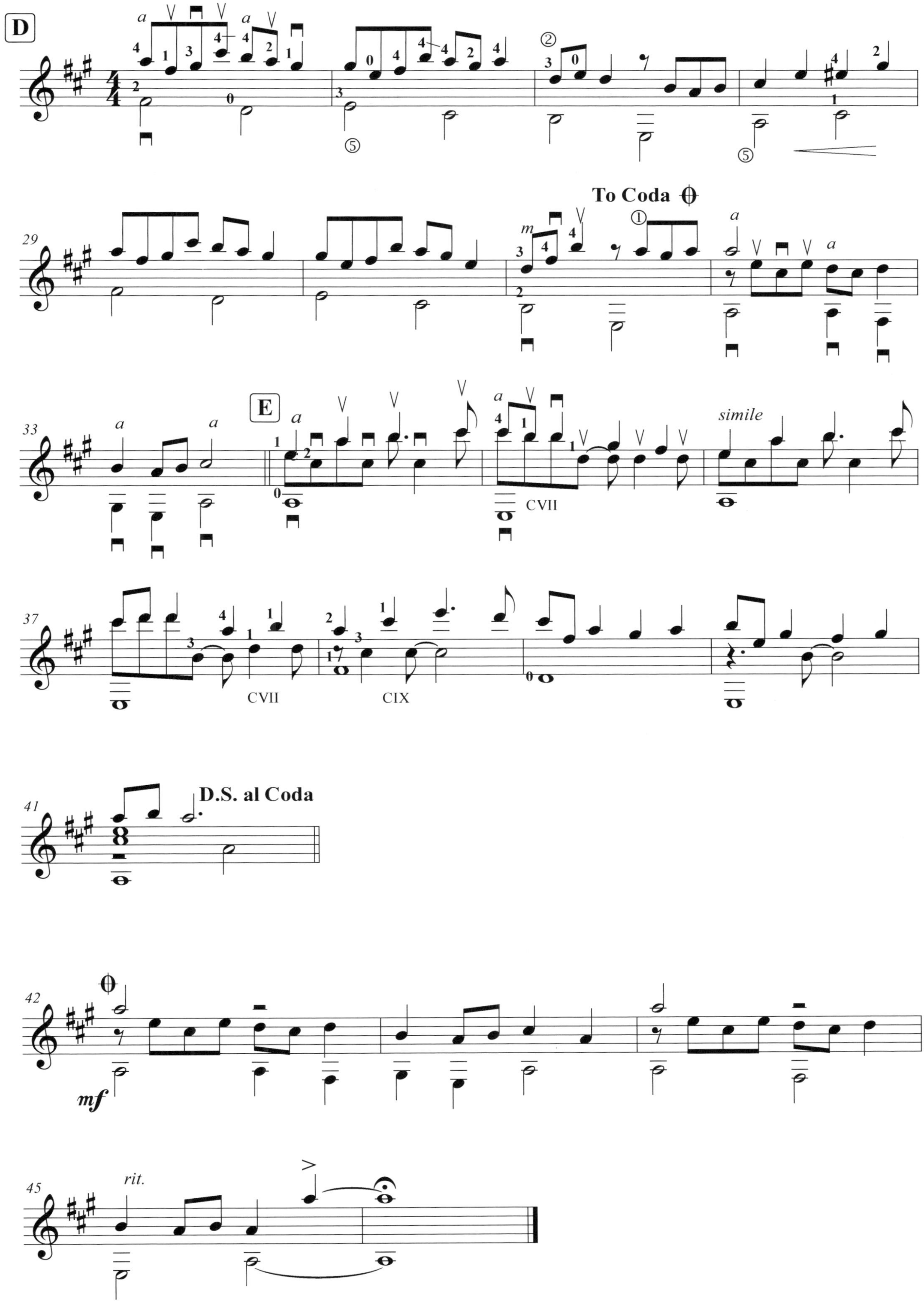
D
To Coda
E
simile
CVII
CIX
D.S. al Coda
mf
rit.

Autumn Soliloquy

♩. = ca. 58 **Spirito**

Sustain bass tones throughout.

Keijo Pennanen

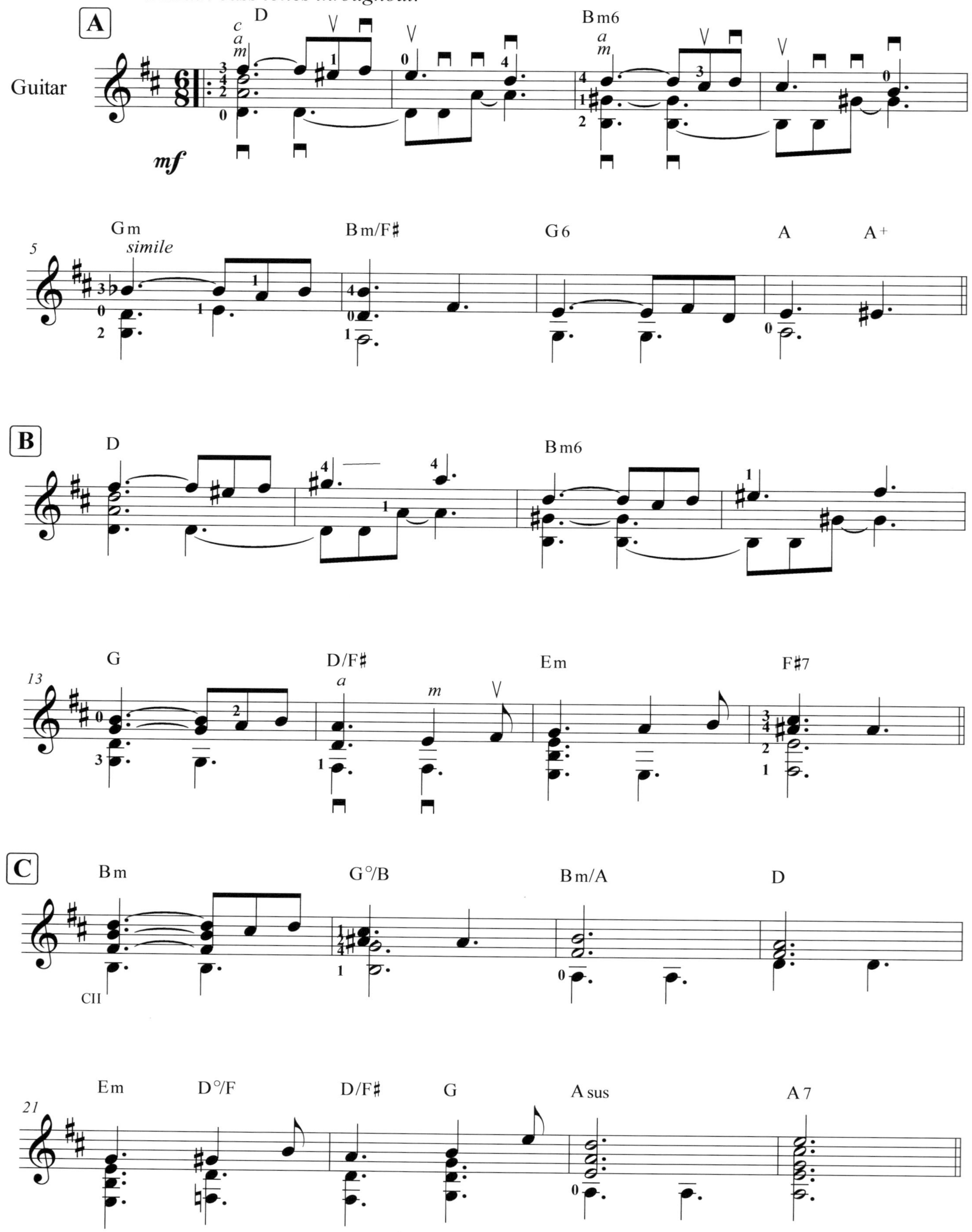

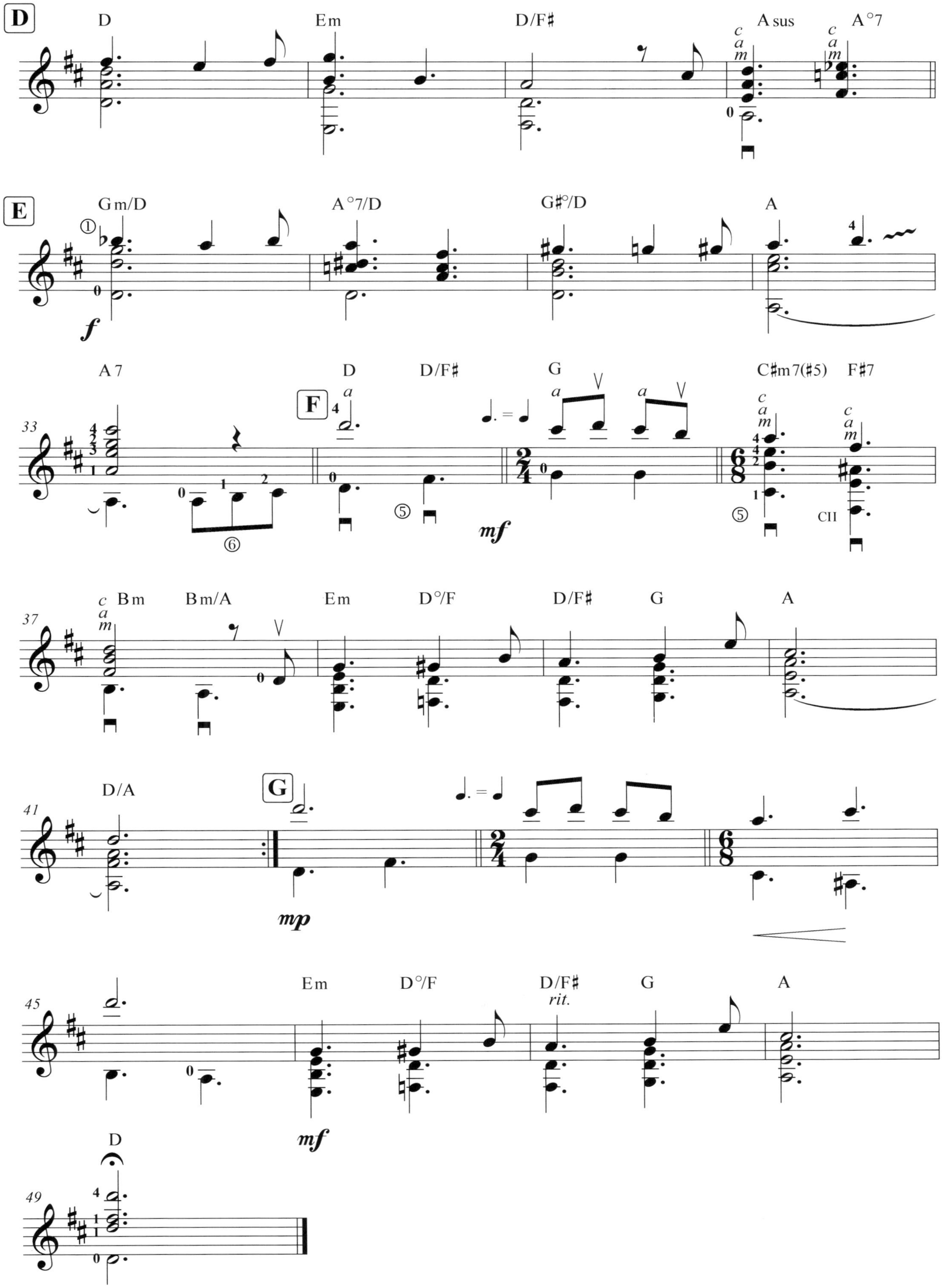
D
D Em D/F♯ A sus A°7
E
Gm/D A°7/D G♯°/D A
f
A7 D D/F♯ G C♯m7(♯5) F♯7
F
mf
CII
Bm Bm/A Em D°/F D/F♯ G A
D/A
G
mp
Em D°/F D/F♯ G A
rit.
mf
D

Spring Views

Andante (♩ = ca. 97)
Dropped-D Tuning

Keijo Pennanen

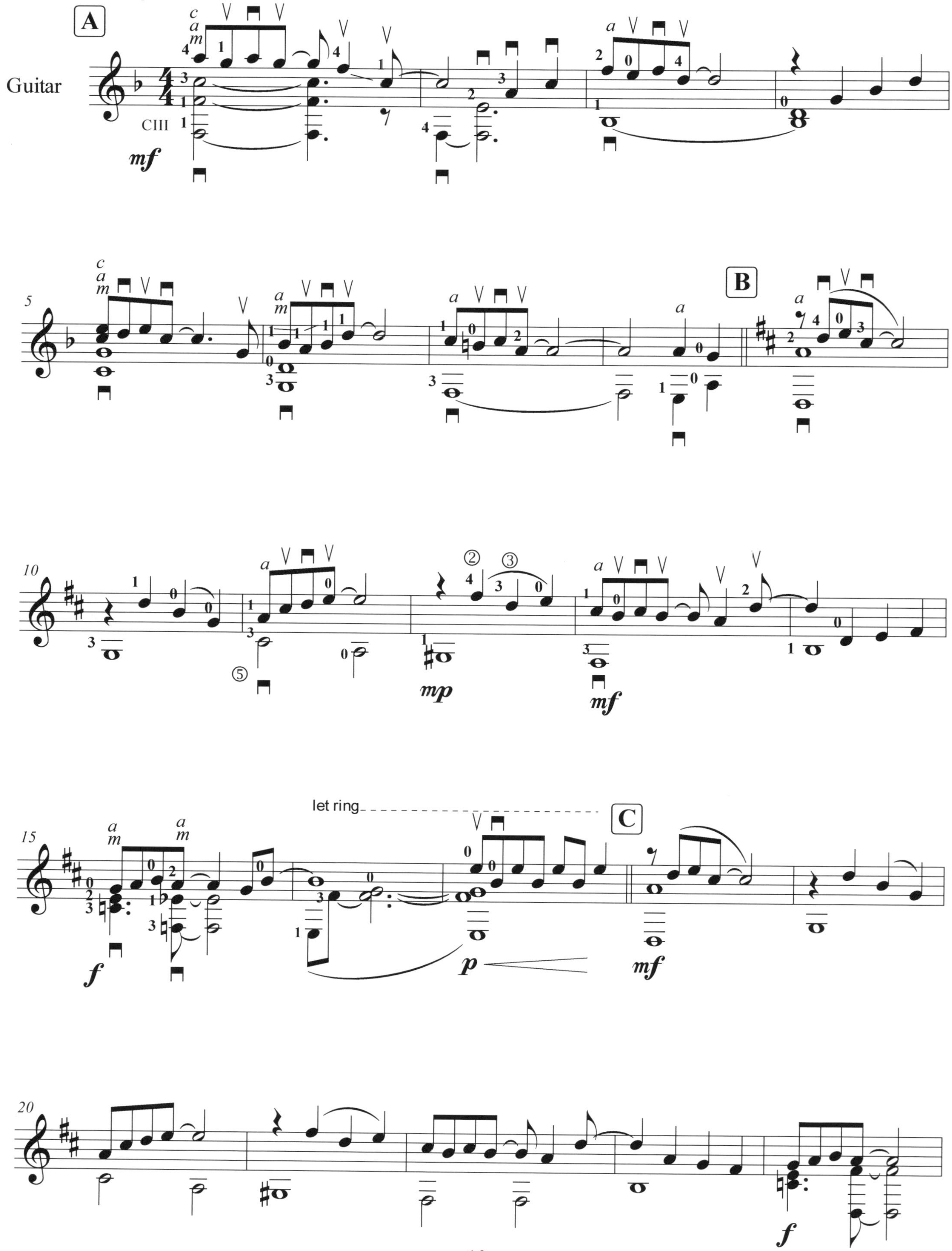

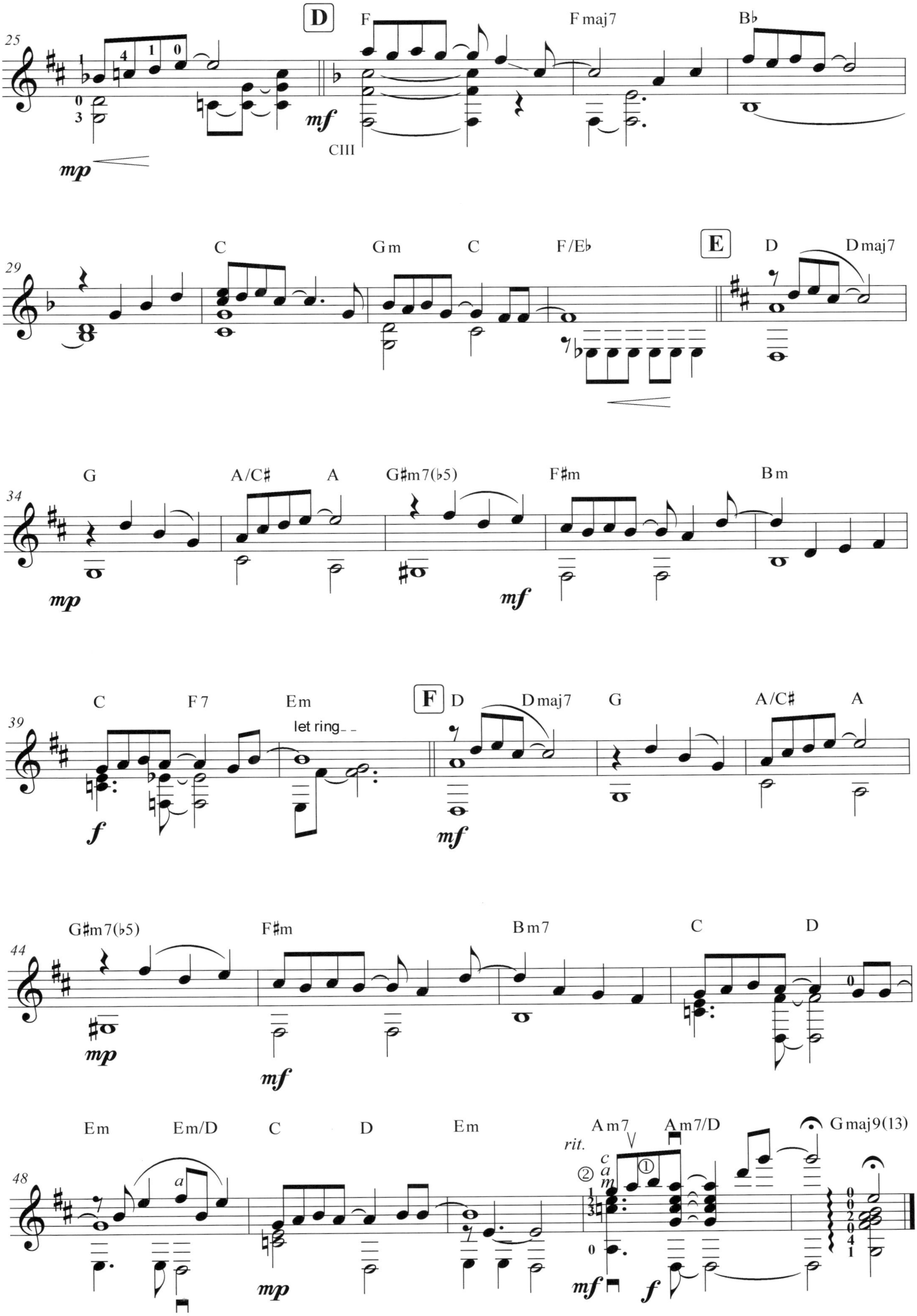
D
F
F maj7
B♭
CIII
C
Gm
C
F/E♭
E
D
D maj7
G
A/C♯
A
G♯m7(♭5)
F♯m
Bm
C
F7
Em
let ring
F
D
D maj7
G
A/C♯
A
G♯m7(♭5)
F♯m
Bm7
C
D
Em
Em/D
C
D
Em
Am7
Am7/D
rit.
G maj9(13)

Dedication

Largo (♩ = ca. 56)

Keijo Pennanen

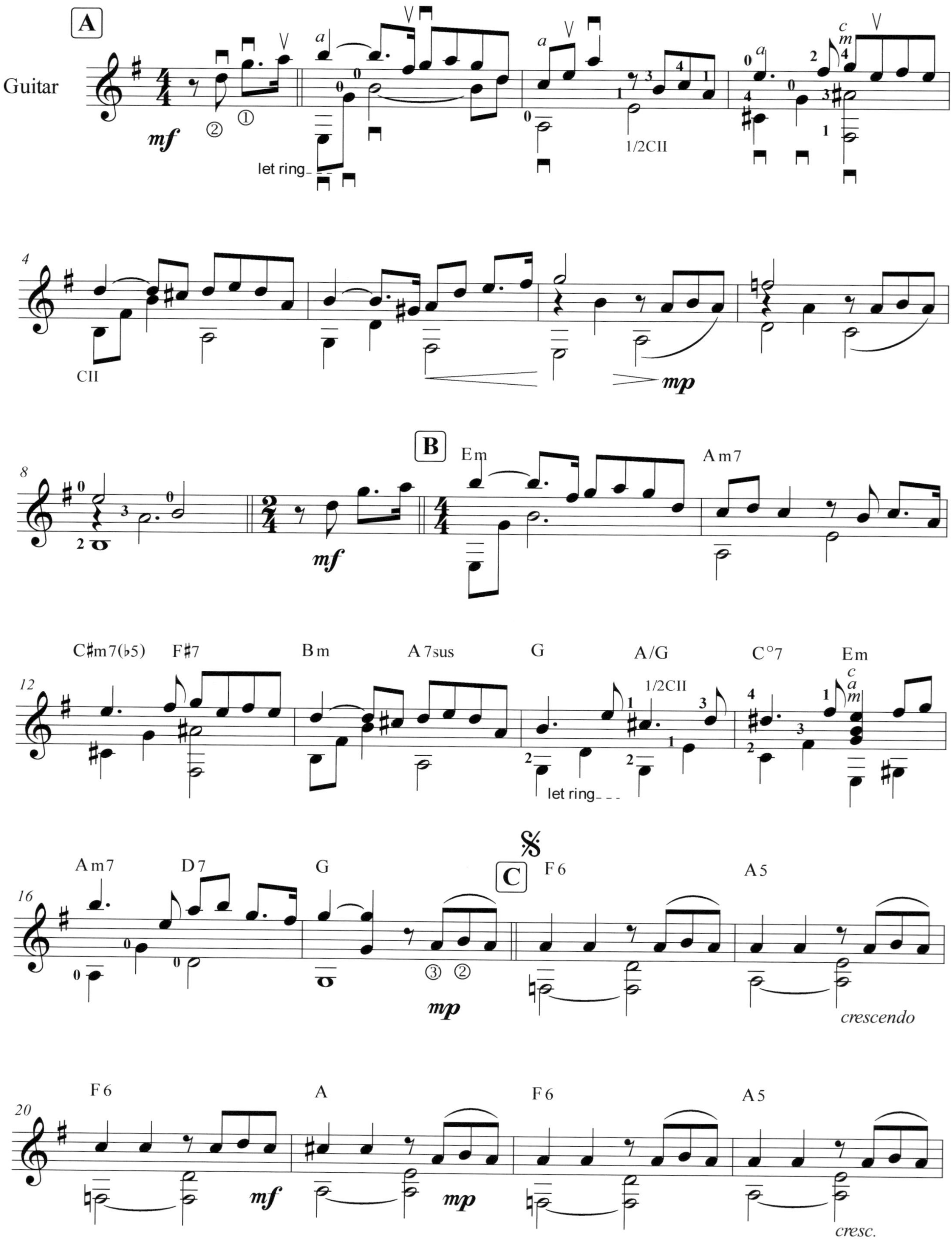

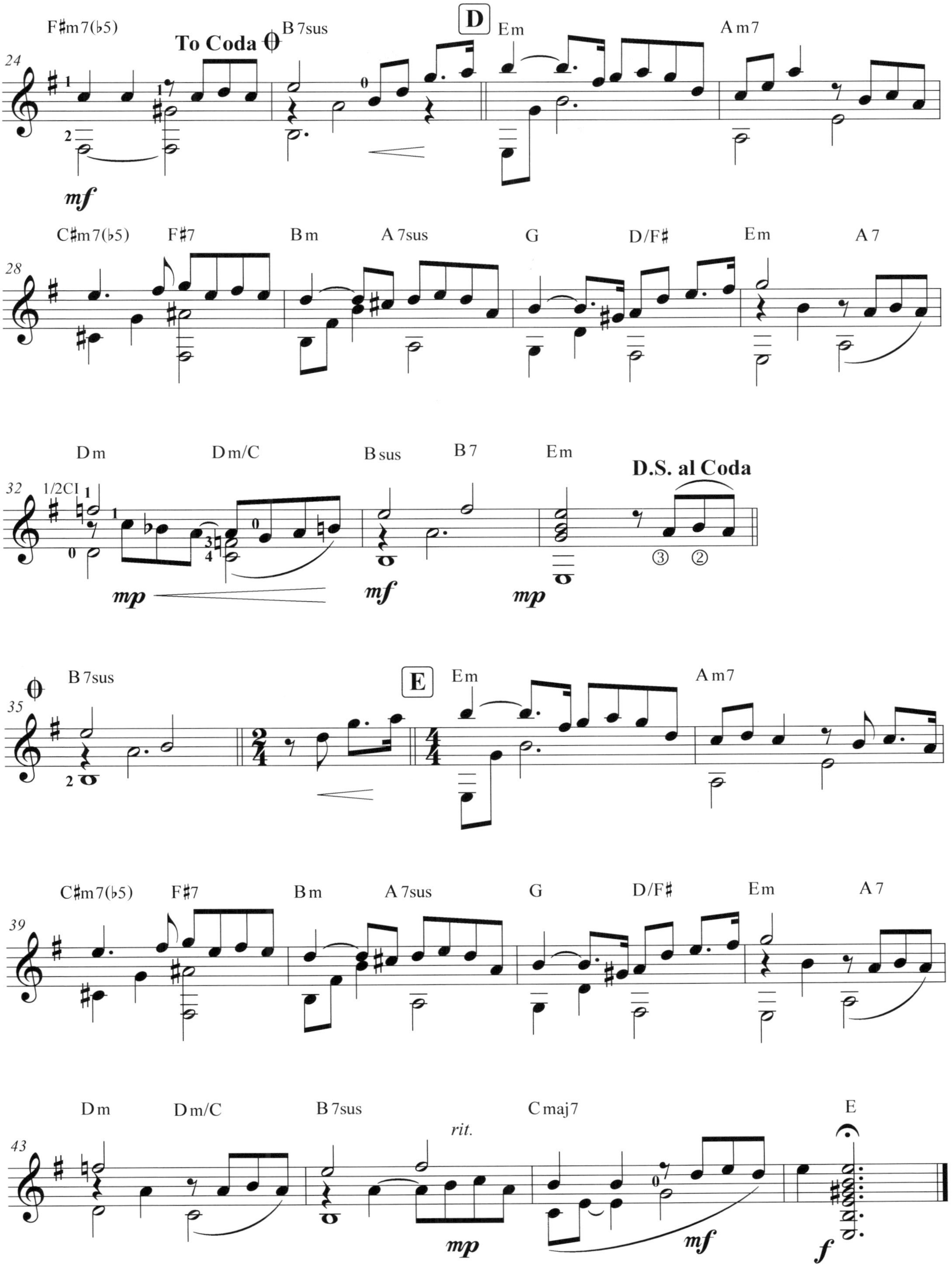
F♯m7(♭5)
To Coda
B 7sus
D
Em
Am7
mf
C♯m7(♭5)
F♯7
Bm
A 7sus
G
D/F♯
Em
A 7
Dm
Dm/C
B sus
B 7
Em
D.S. al Coda
1/2CI
mp
mf
mp
B 7sus
E
Em
Am7
C♯m7(♭5)
F♯7
Bm
A 7sus
G
D/F♯
Em
A 7
Dm
Dm/C
B 7sus
rit.
Cmaj7
E
mp
mf
f

Navigator

Adagio(♩ = ca. 75)

Keijo Pennanen

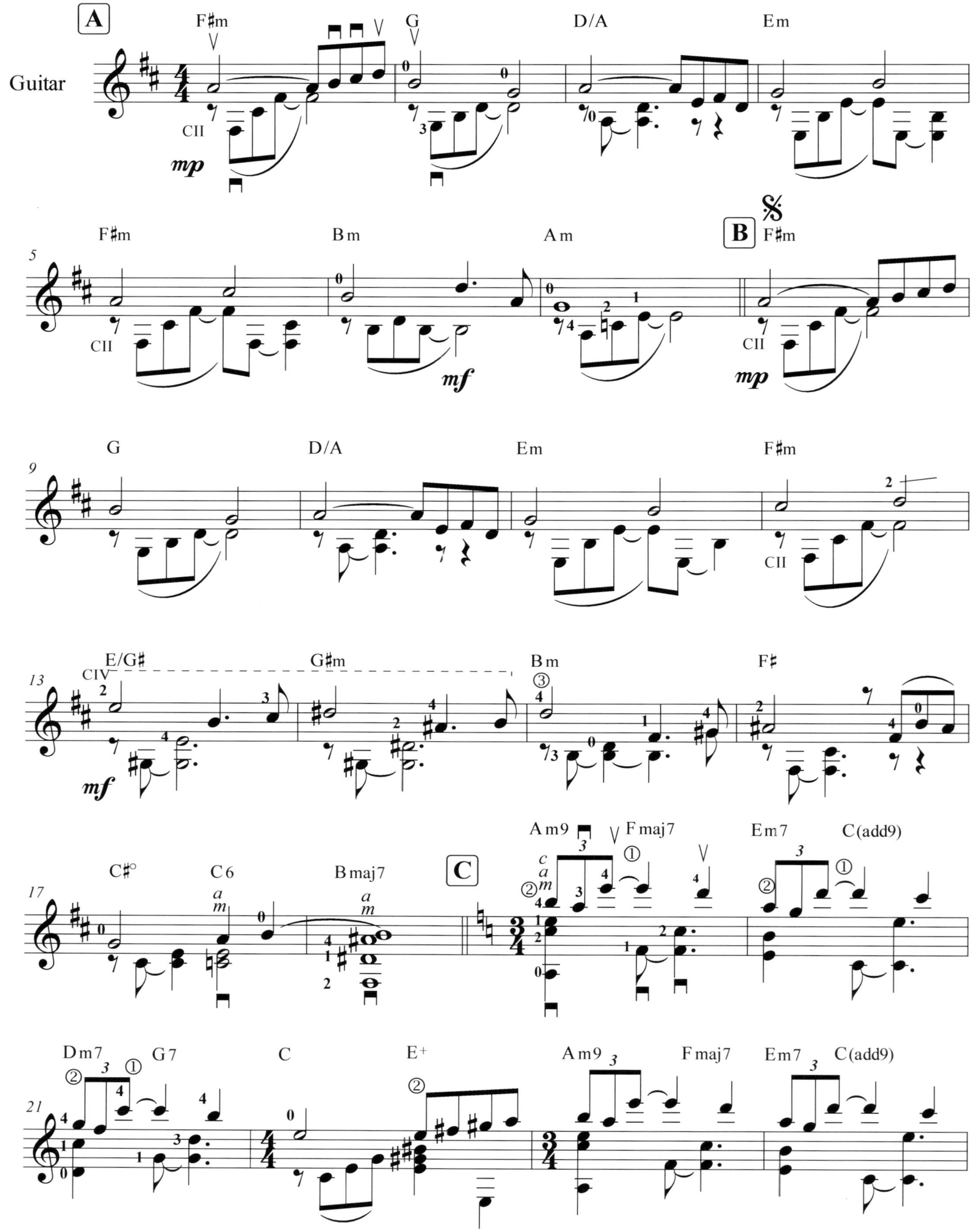

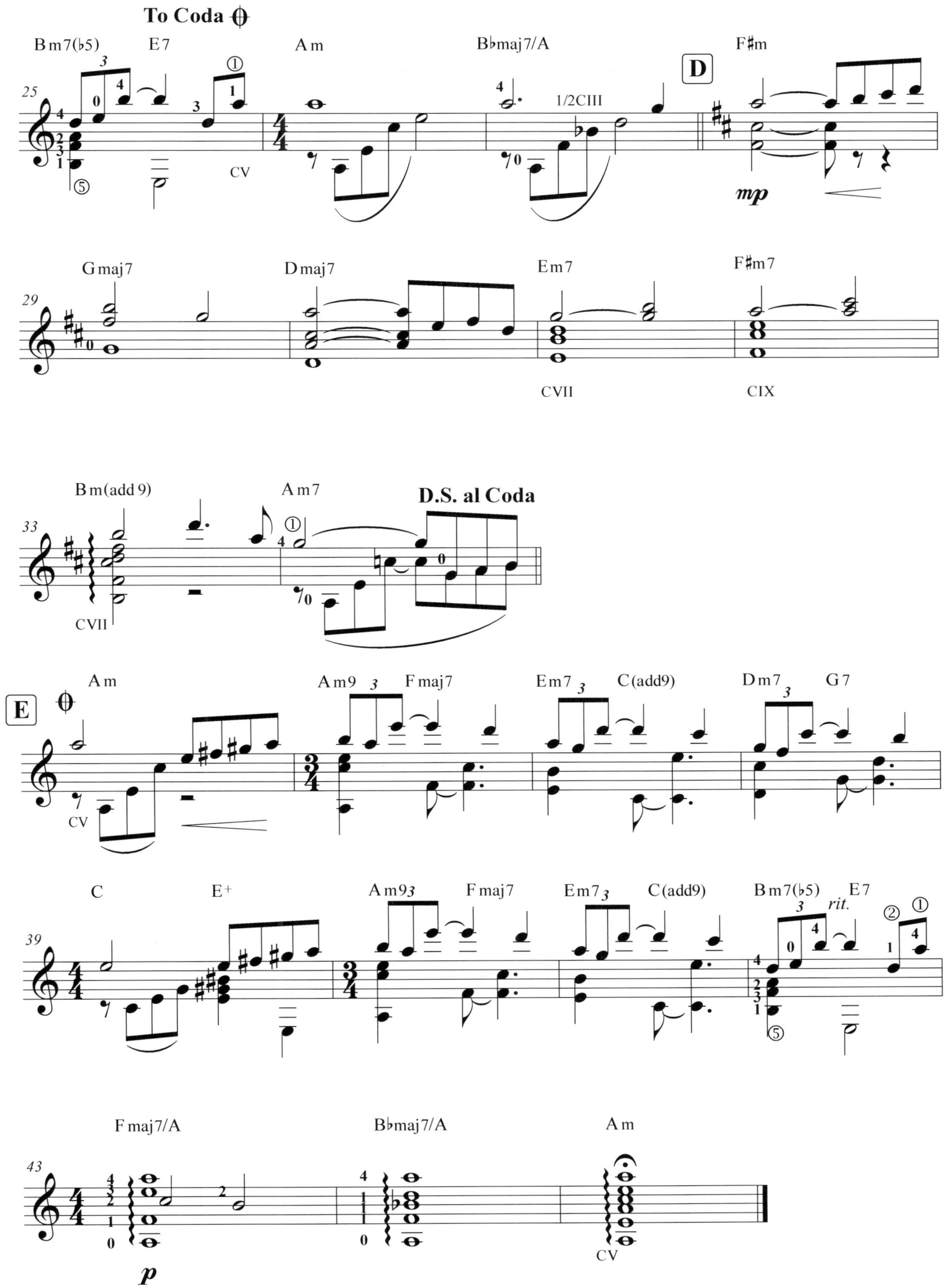
To Coda
Bm7(♭5)
E7
Am
B♭maj7/A
F♯m
D
1/2CIII
CV
mp
Gmaj7
Dmaj7
Em7
F♯m7
CVII
CIX
Bm(add 9)
Am7
D.S. al Coda
CVII
E
Am
Am9
Fmaj7
Em7
C(add9)
Dm7
G7
CV
C
E+
Am9
Fmaj7
Em7
C(add9)
Bm7(♭5)
E7
rit.
Fmaj7/A
B♭maj7/A
Am
p
CV

Chordinator

Allegro vivace

Keijo Pennanen

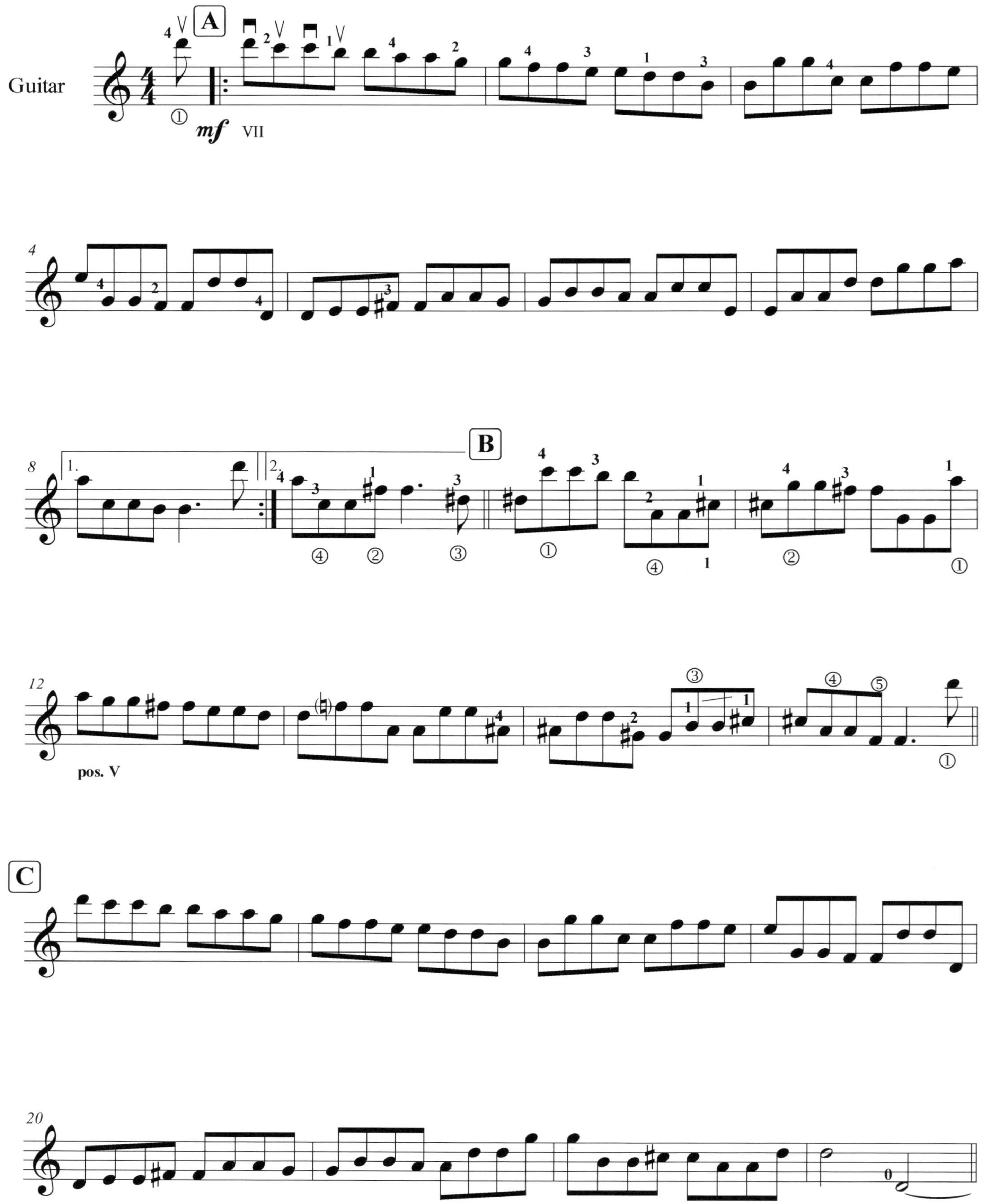

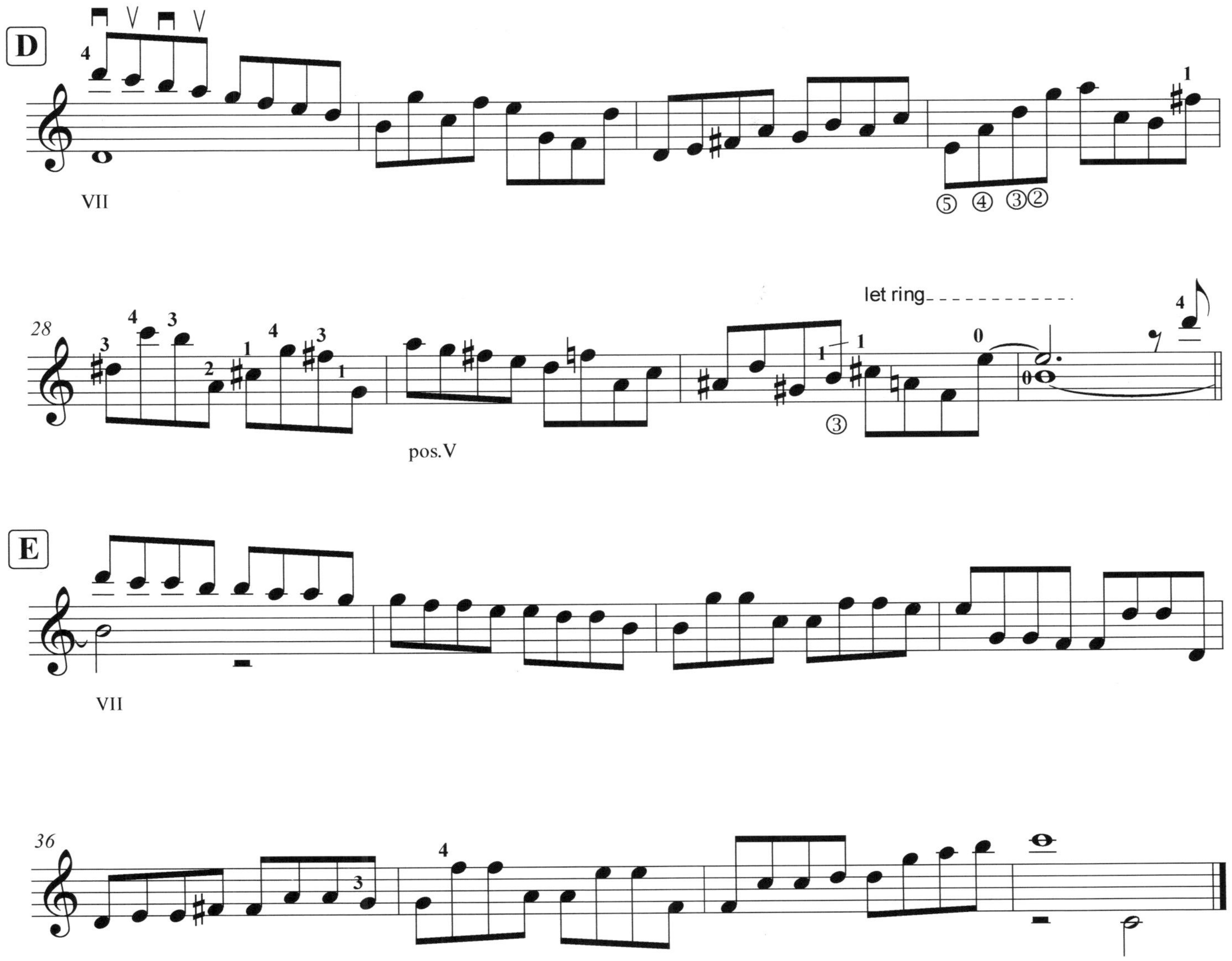
D
VII
⑤ ④ ③②
28
pos.V
let ring
③
E
VII
36

On the Move

Bossa (♩ = ca. 63)

Keijo Pennanen

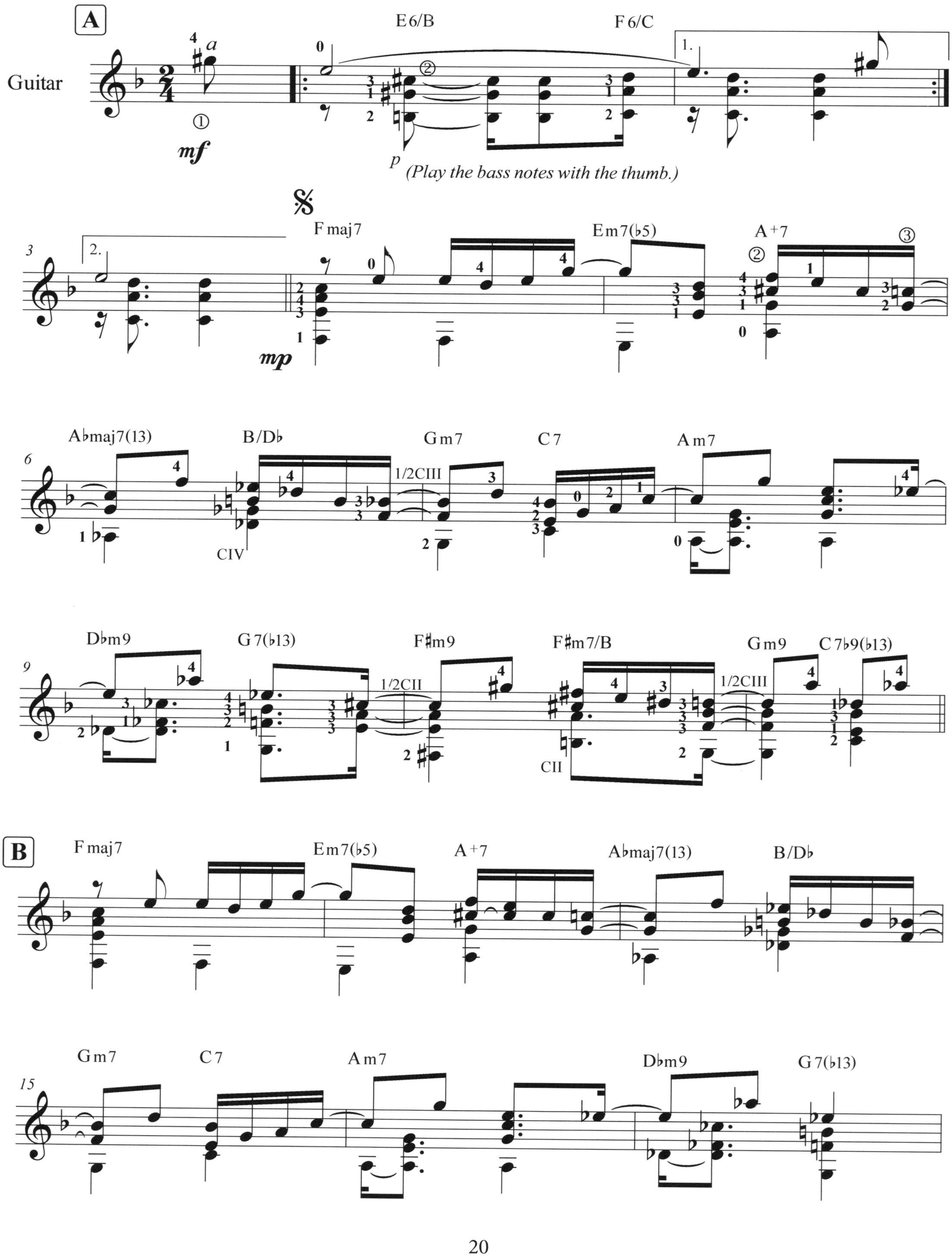

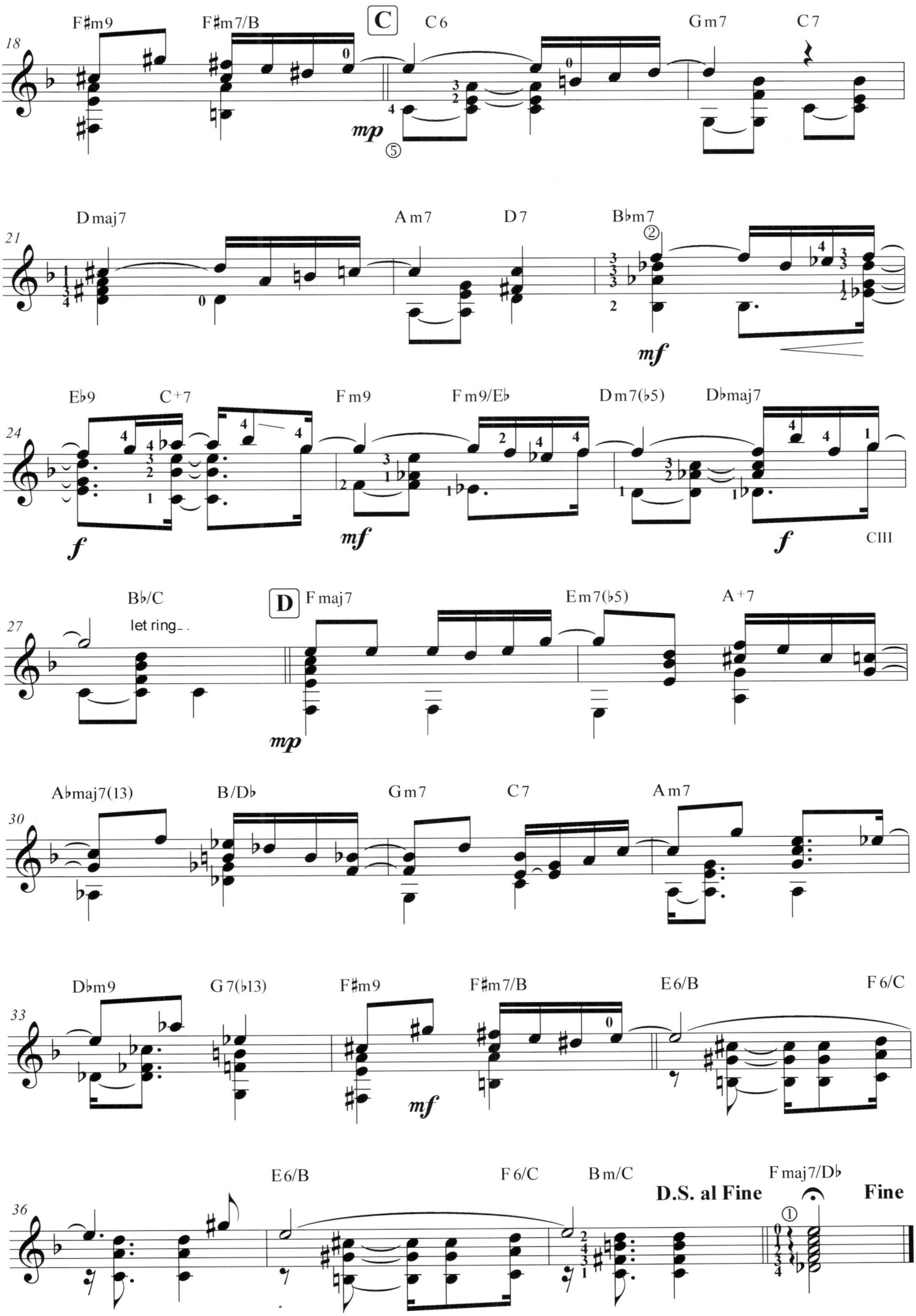

F♯m9 F♯m7/B C C6 Gm7 C7
mp
D maj7 Am7 D7 B♭m7
mf
E♭9 C+7 Fm9 Fm9/E♭ Dm7(♭5) D♭maj7
f mf f CIII
B♭/C let ring D Fmaj7 Em7(♭5) A+7
mp
A♭maj7(13) B/D♭ Gm7 C7 Am7
D♭m9 G7(♭13) F♯m9 F♯m7/B E6/B F6/C
mf
E6/B F6/C Bm/C D.S. al Fine Fmaj7/D♭ Fine

10

Family Tree

Adagio (♩ = ca. 76)

Keijo Pennanen

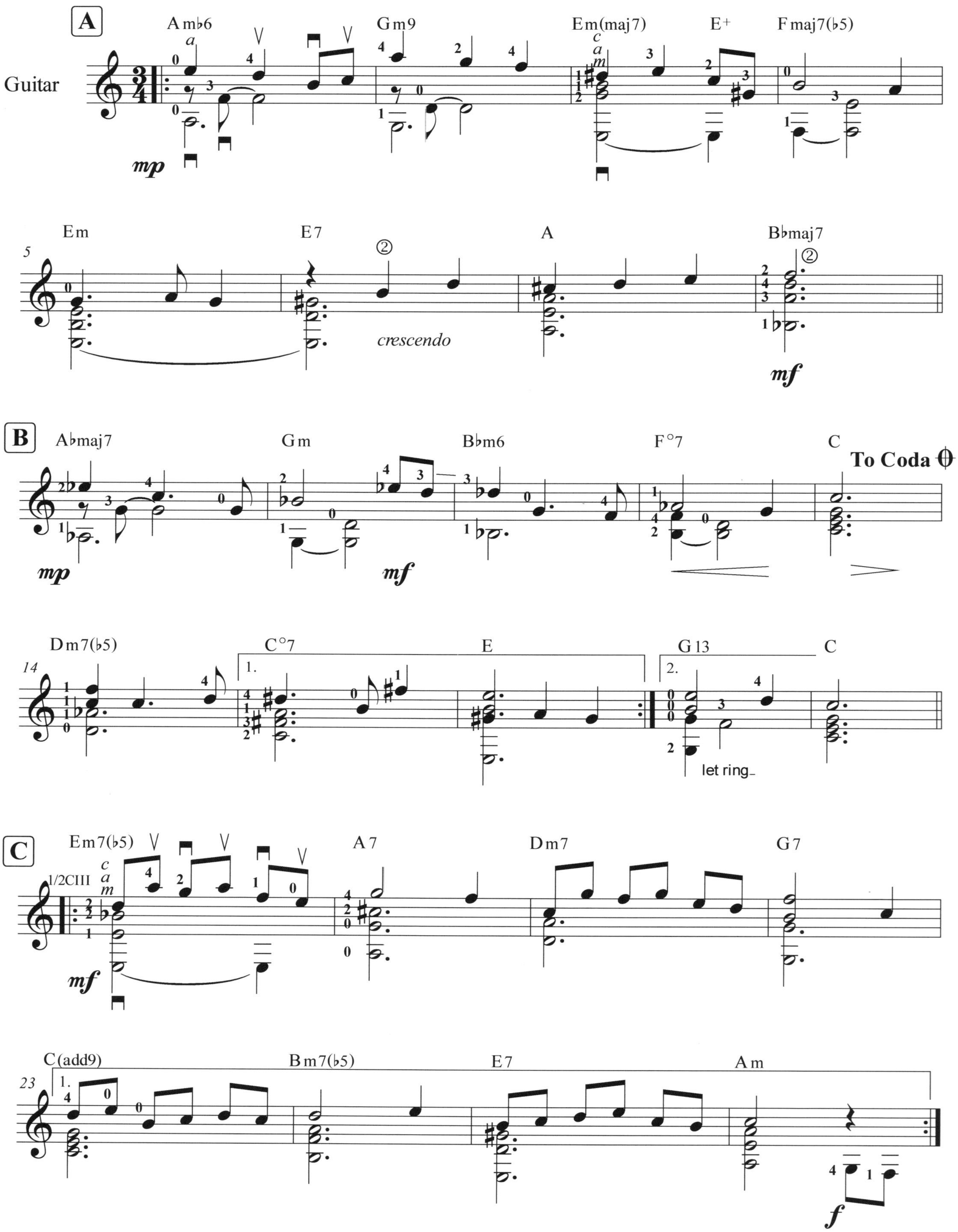

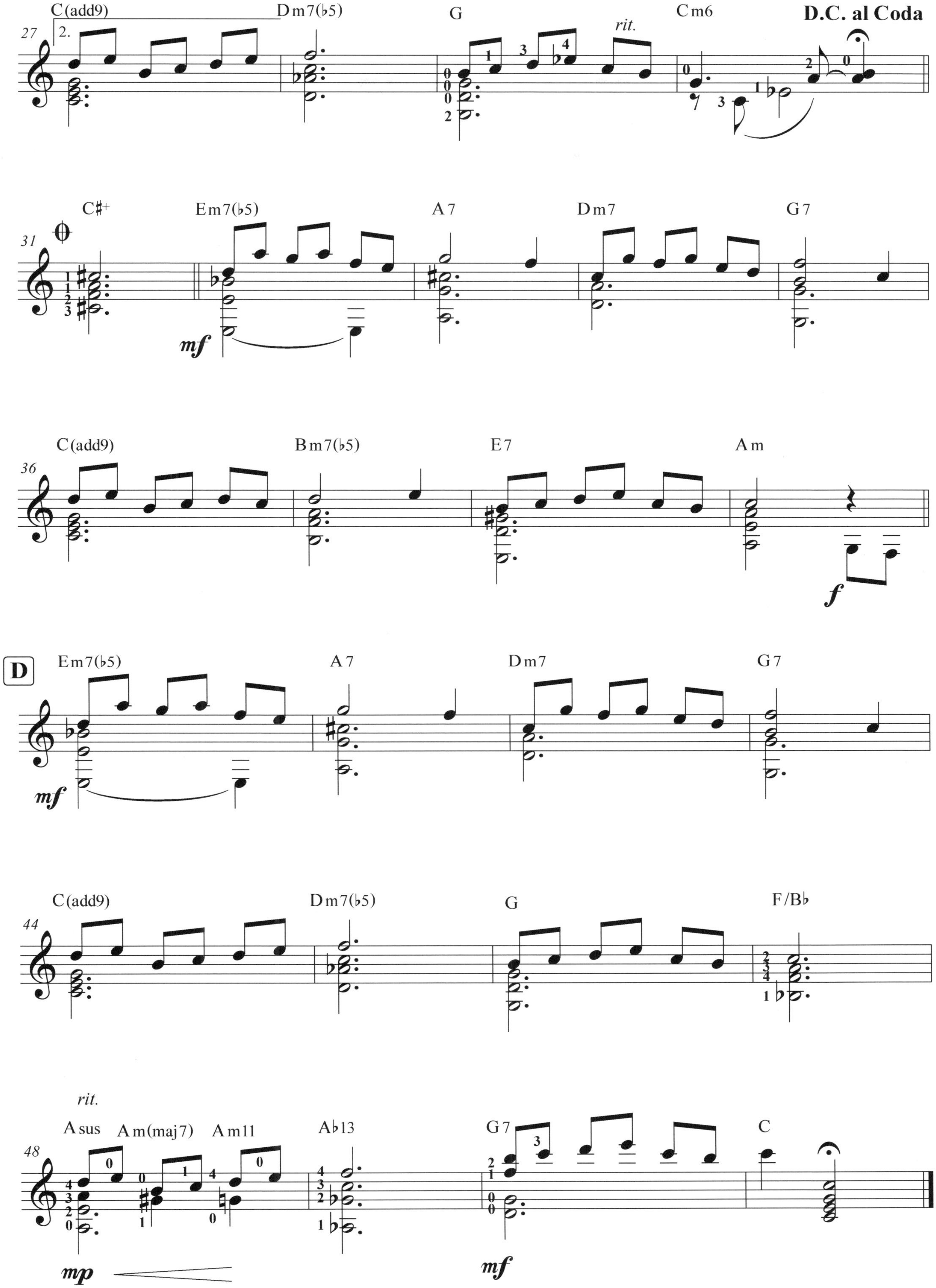
C(add9) 2. Dm7(♭5) G rit. Cm6
D.C. al Coda
C♯+ Em7(♭5) A7 Dm7 G7
mf
C(add9) Bm7(♭5) E7 Am
f
D
Em7(♭5) A7 Dm7 G7
mf
C(add9) Dm7(♭5) G F/B♭
rit.
Asus Am(maj7) Am11 A♭13 G7 C
mp
mf

11

The Old Neighborhood

Medium Swing ♫ = ♩³♪

Keijo Pennanen

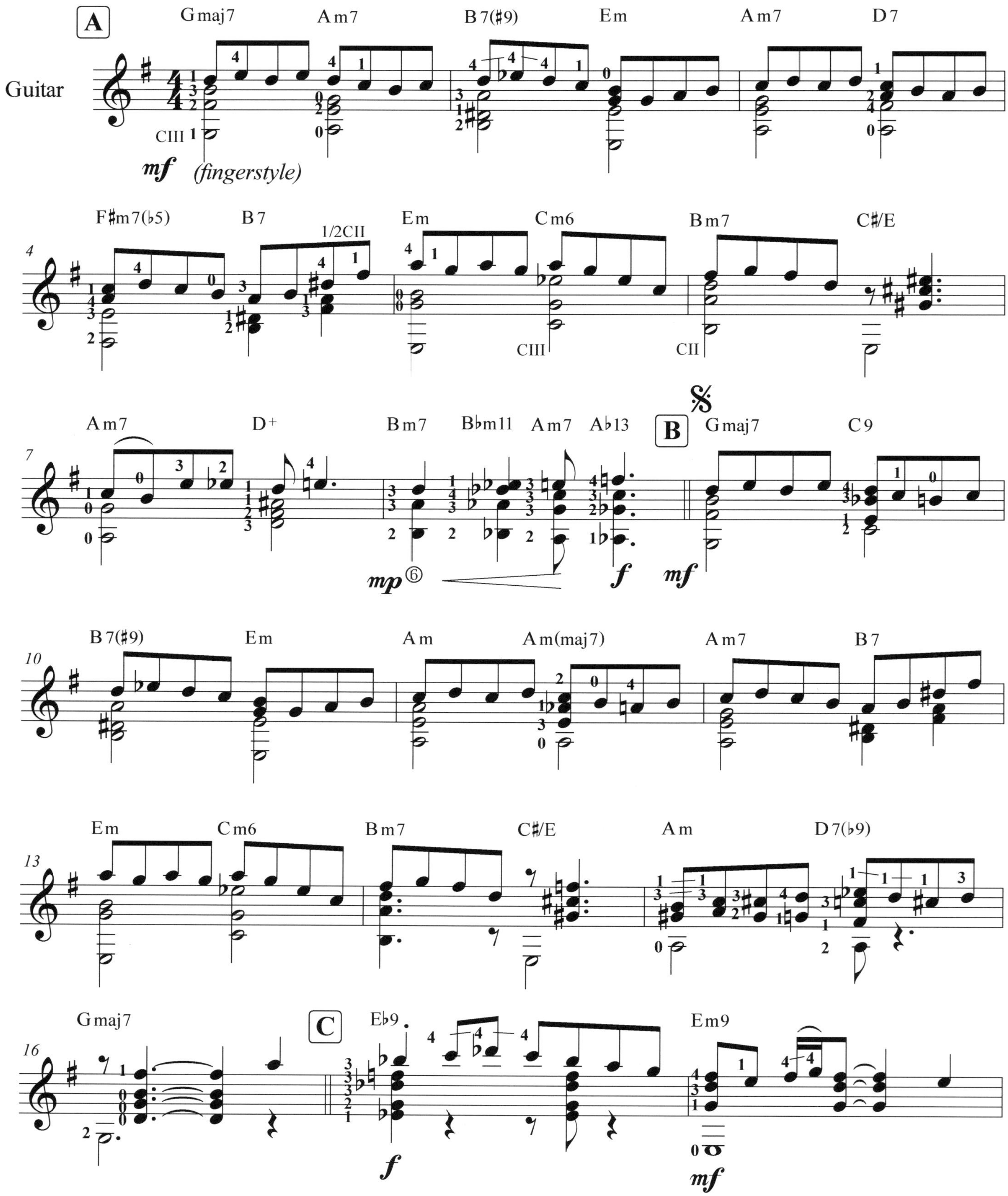

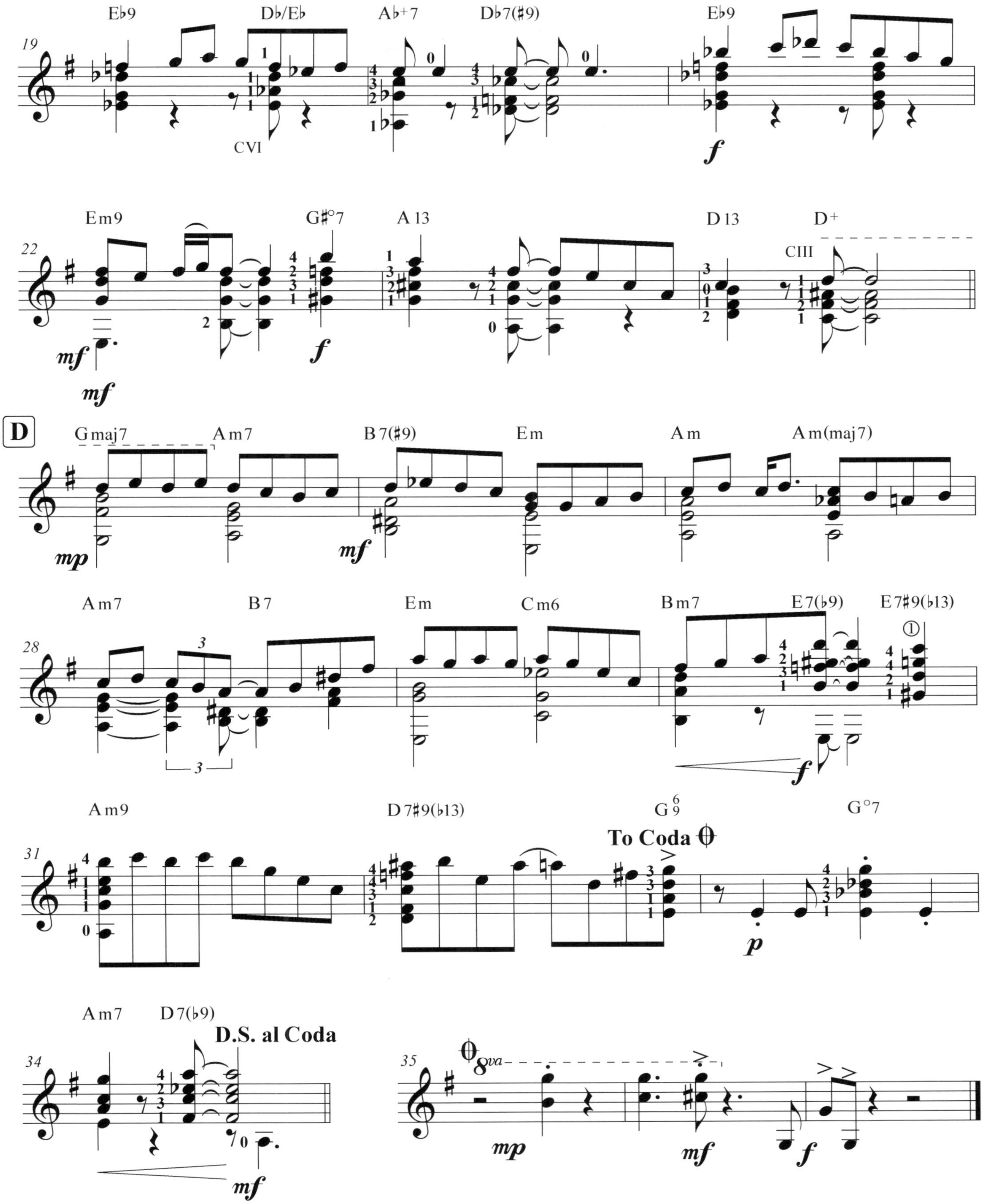

Optionally go to Solo Chorus on the next page.

The Old Neighborhood Solo Chorus

Medium Swing

Keijo Pennanen

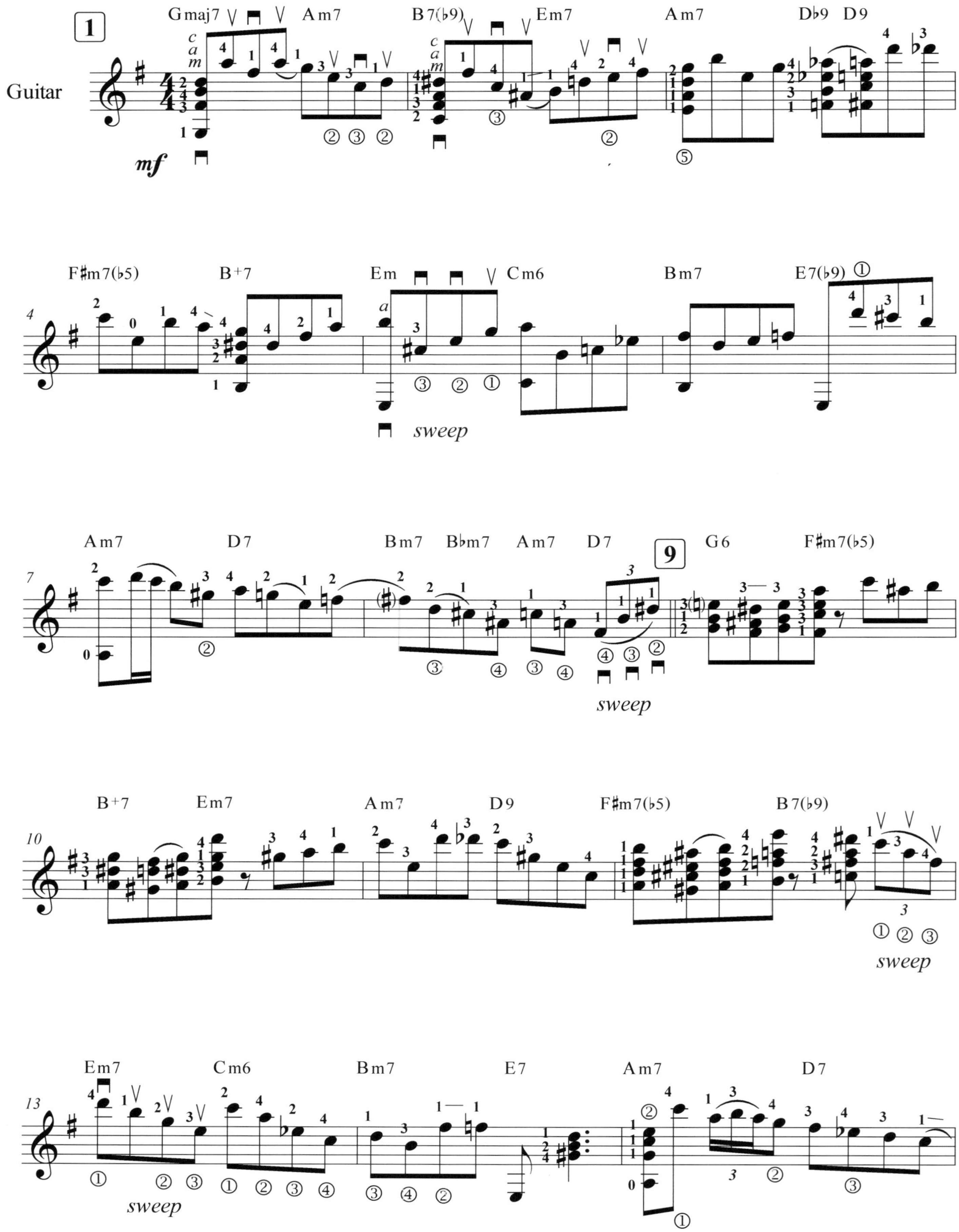

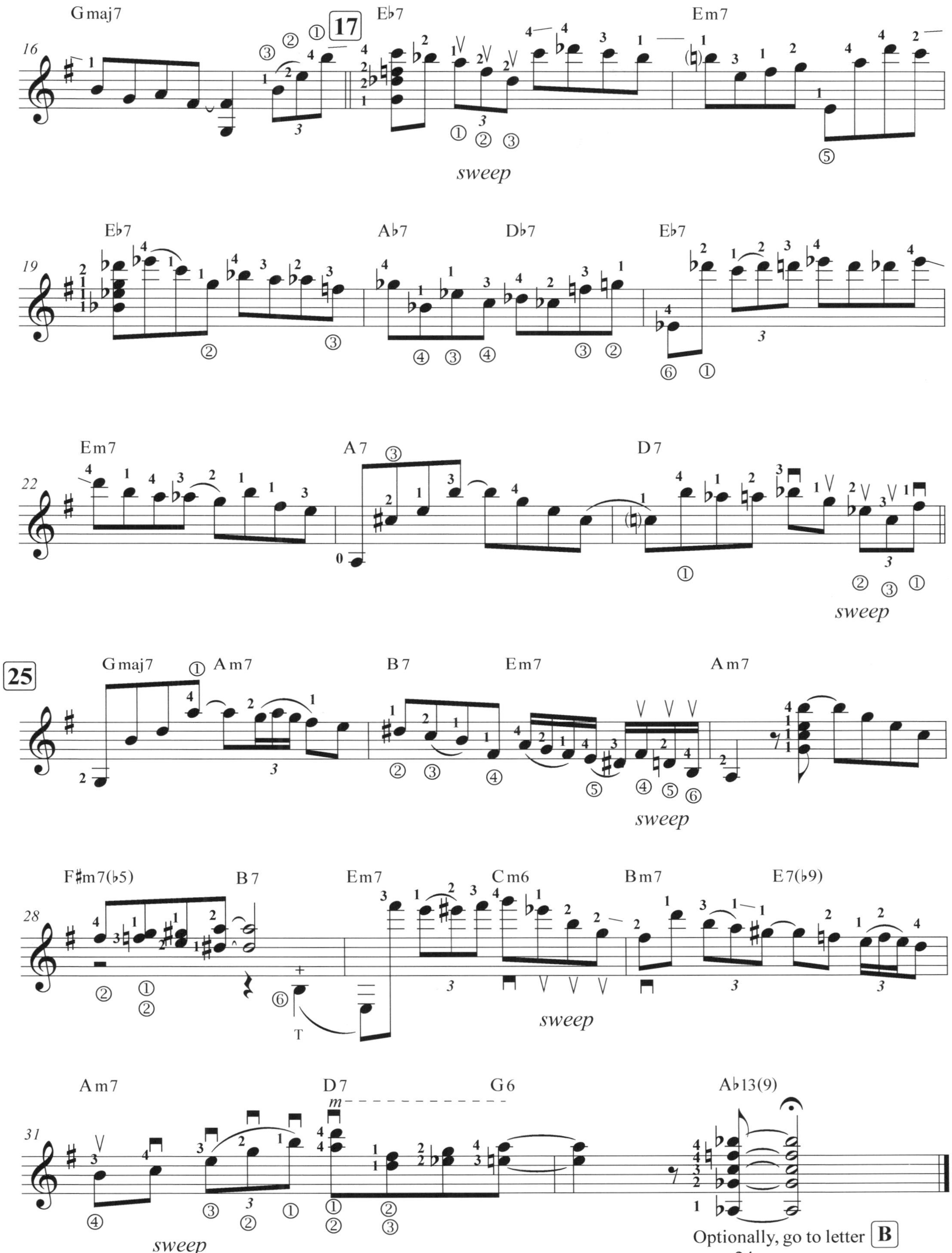

Optionally, go to letter **B** on p. 24.

Forest Play

Allegro (♩ = ca. 126)

Keijo Pennanen

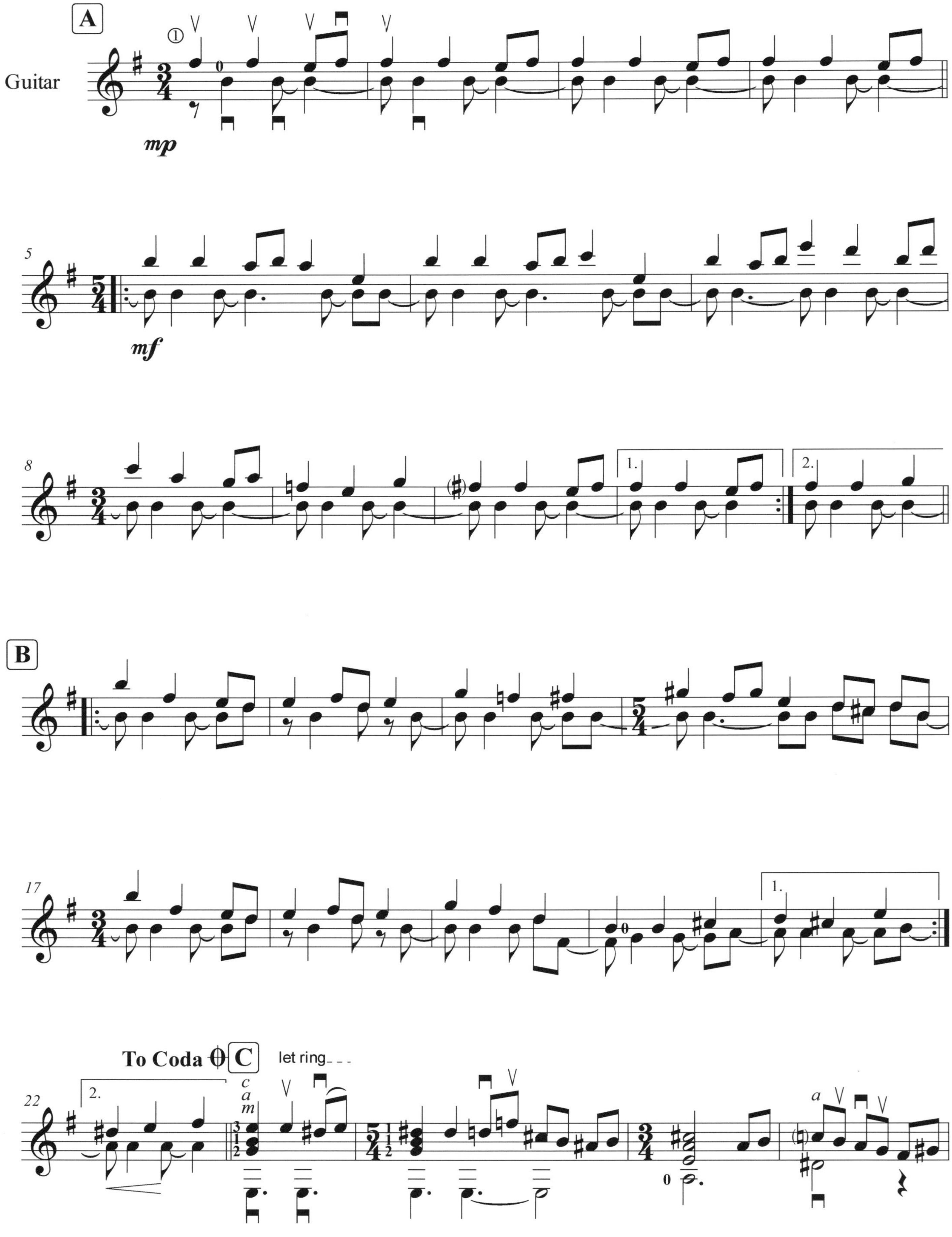

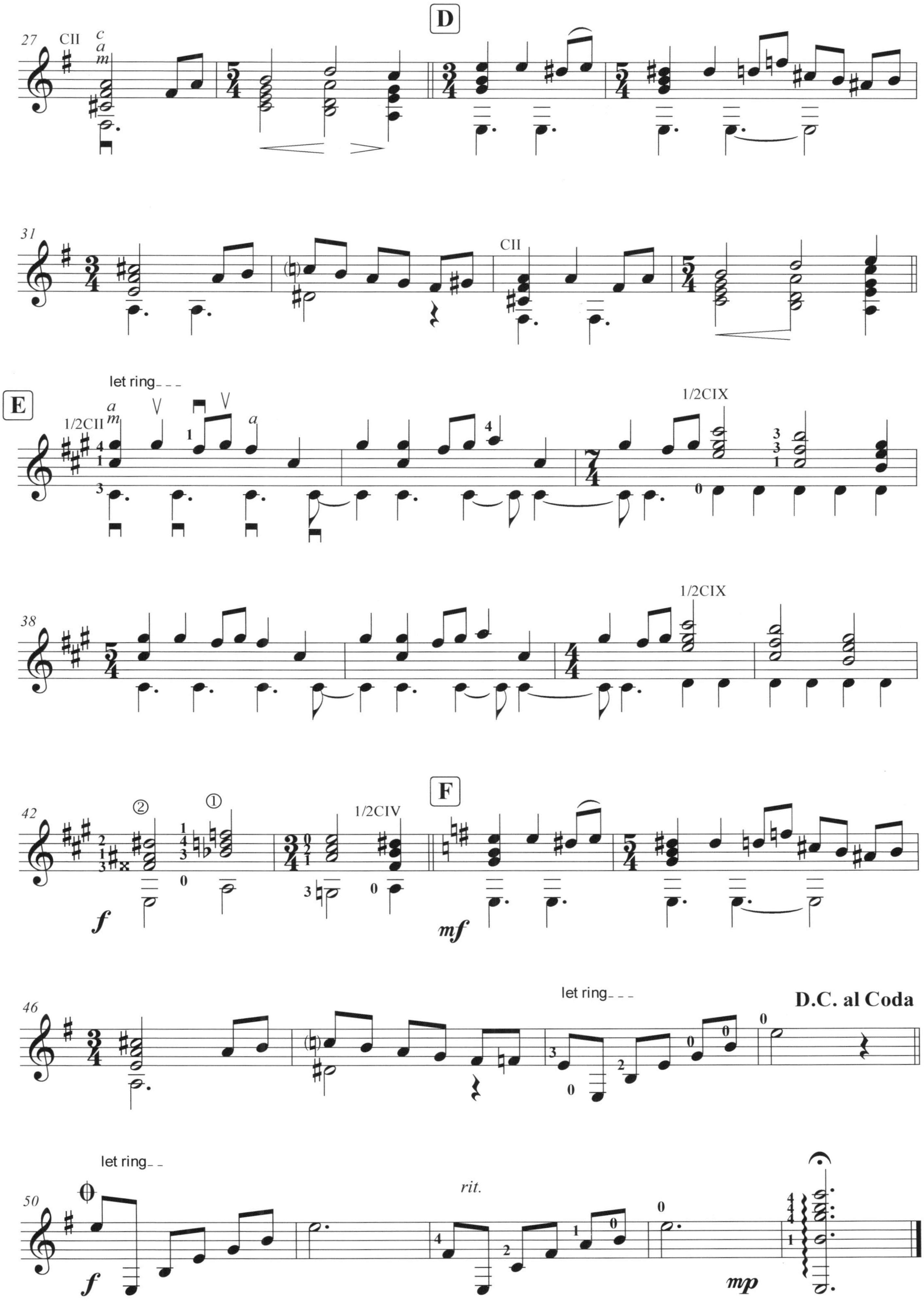
D
CII
E
let ring
1/2CII
1/2CIX
F
1/2CIV
D.C. al Coda
rit.

14

Island Tones

Adagio (♩ = c. 56)

Keijo Pennanen

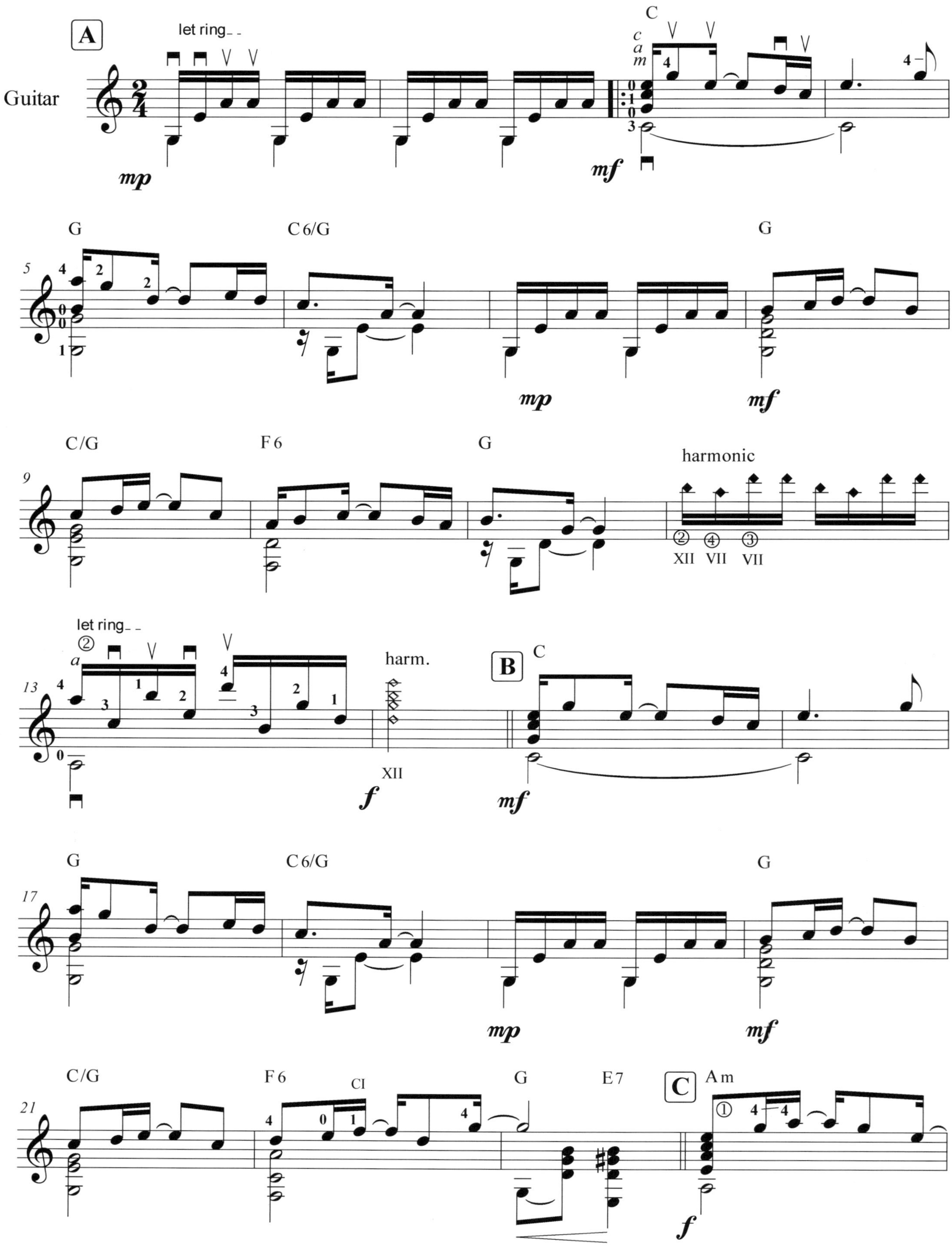

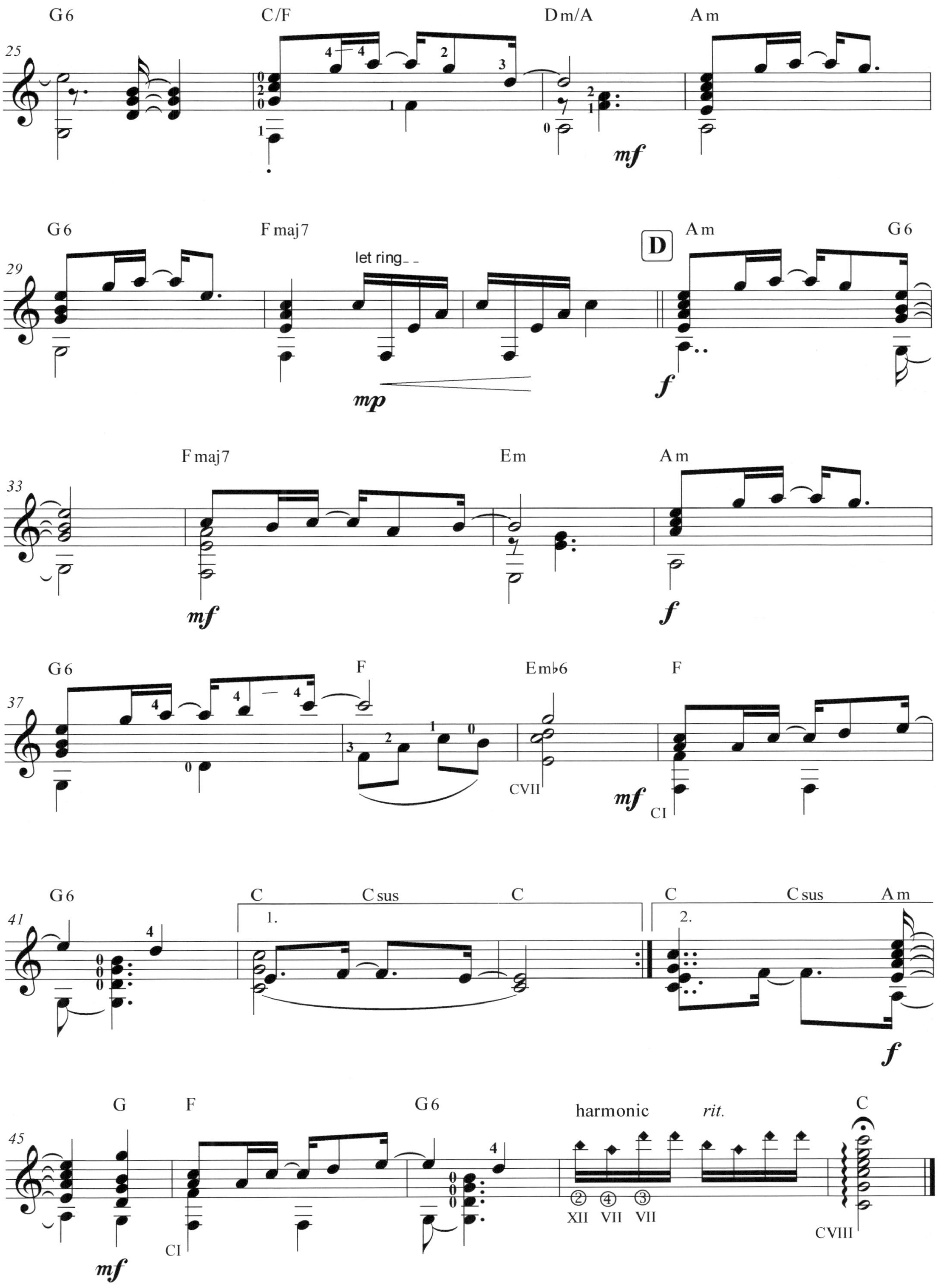
G6
C/F
Dm/A
Am
mf
G6
Fmaj7
let ring
D
Am
G6
mp
f
Fmaj7
Em
Am
mf
f
G6
F
Em♭6
F
CVII
mf
CI
G6
C
Csus
C
1.
C
Csus
Am
2.
f
G
F
G6
harmonic
rit.
C
XII
VII
VII
CVIII
CI
mf

Stairway of Time

Adagio (♩ = ca. 76)

Keijo Pennanen

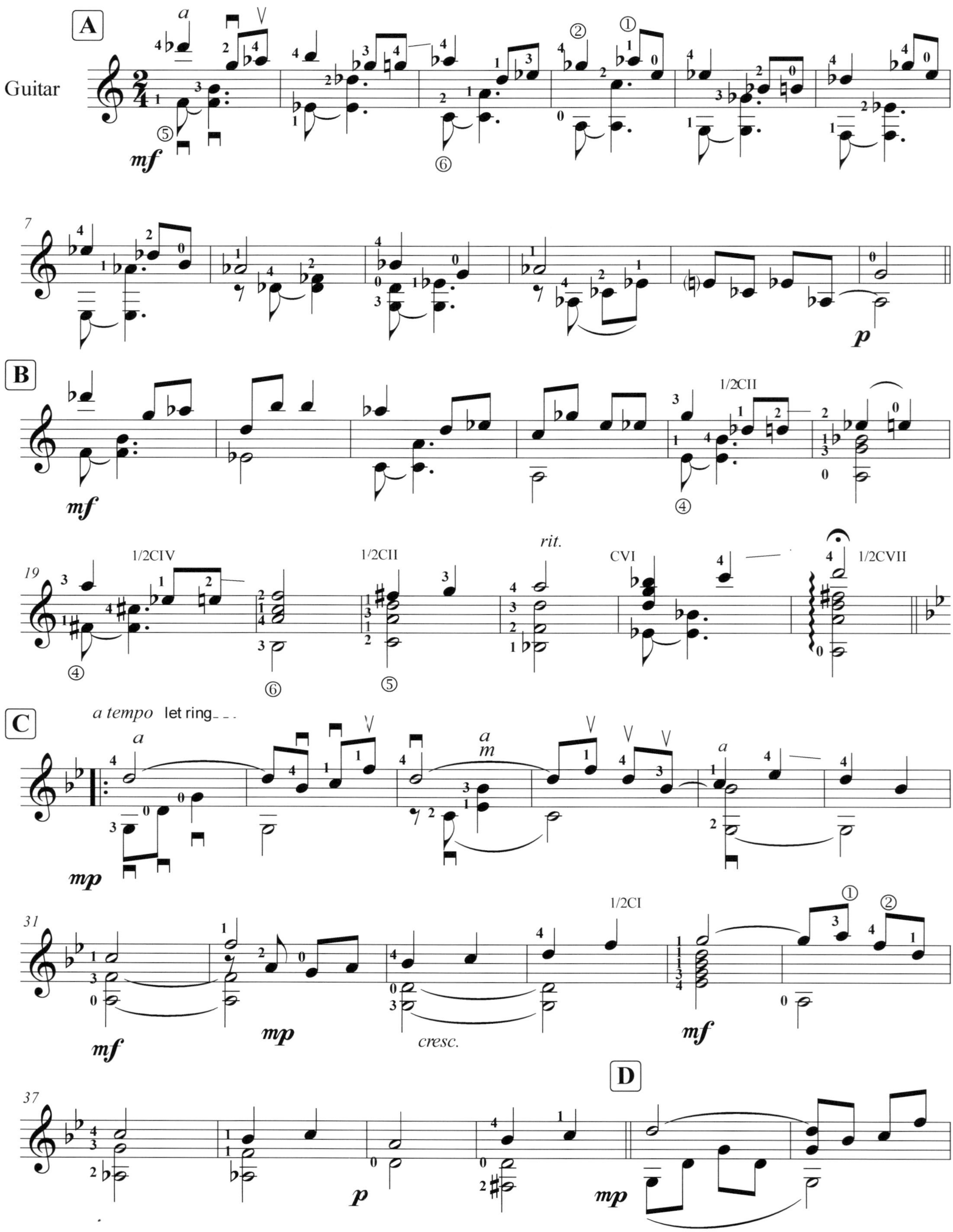

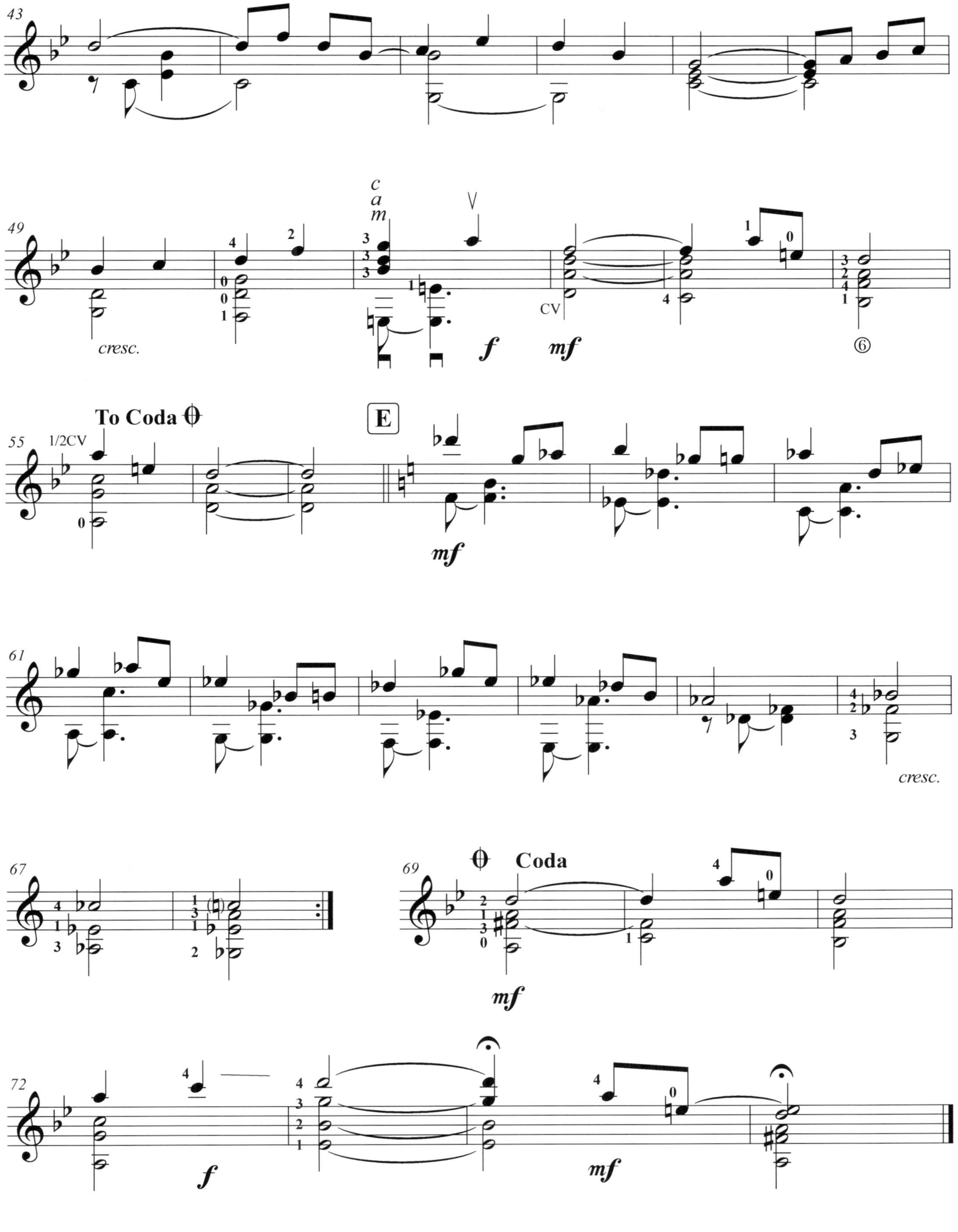
cresc.
f
mf
CV
To Coda
1/2CV
E
mf
cresc.
Coda
mf
f
mf

16

Outbound Shuffle

Funky Swing (♩ = ca. 84)

Keijo Pennanen

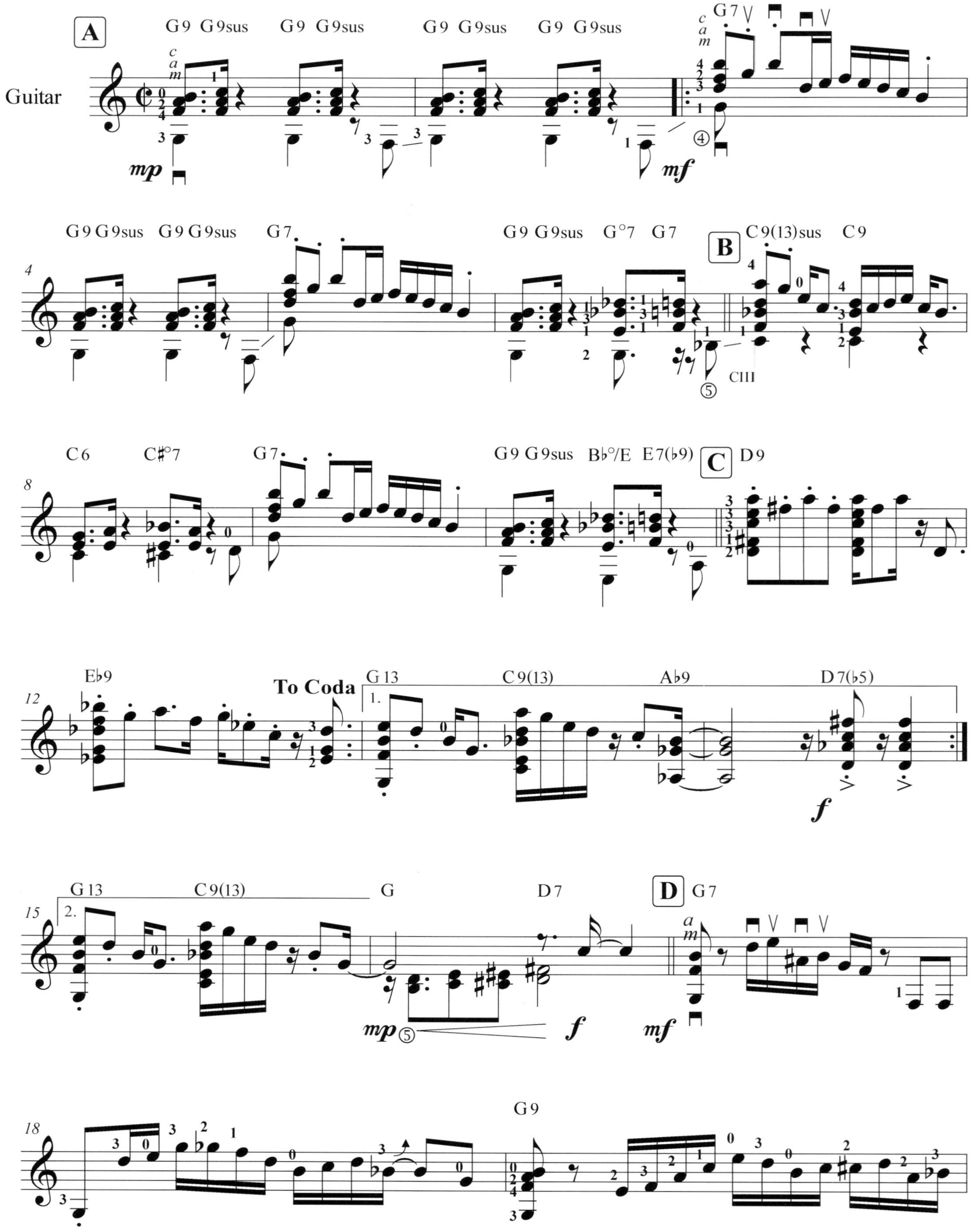

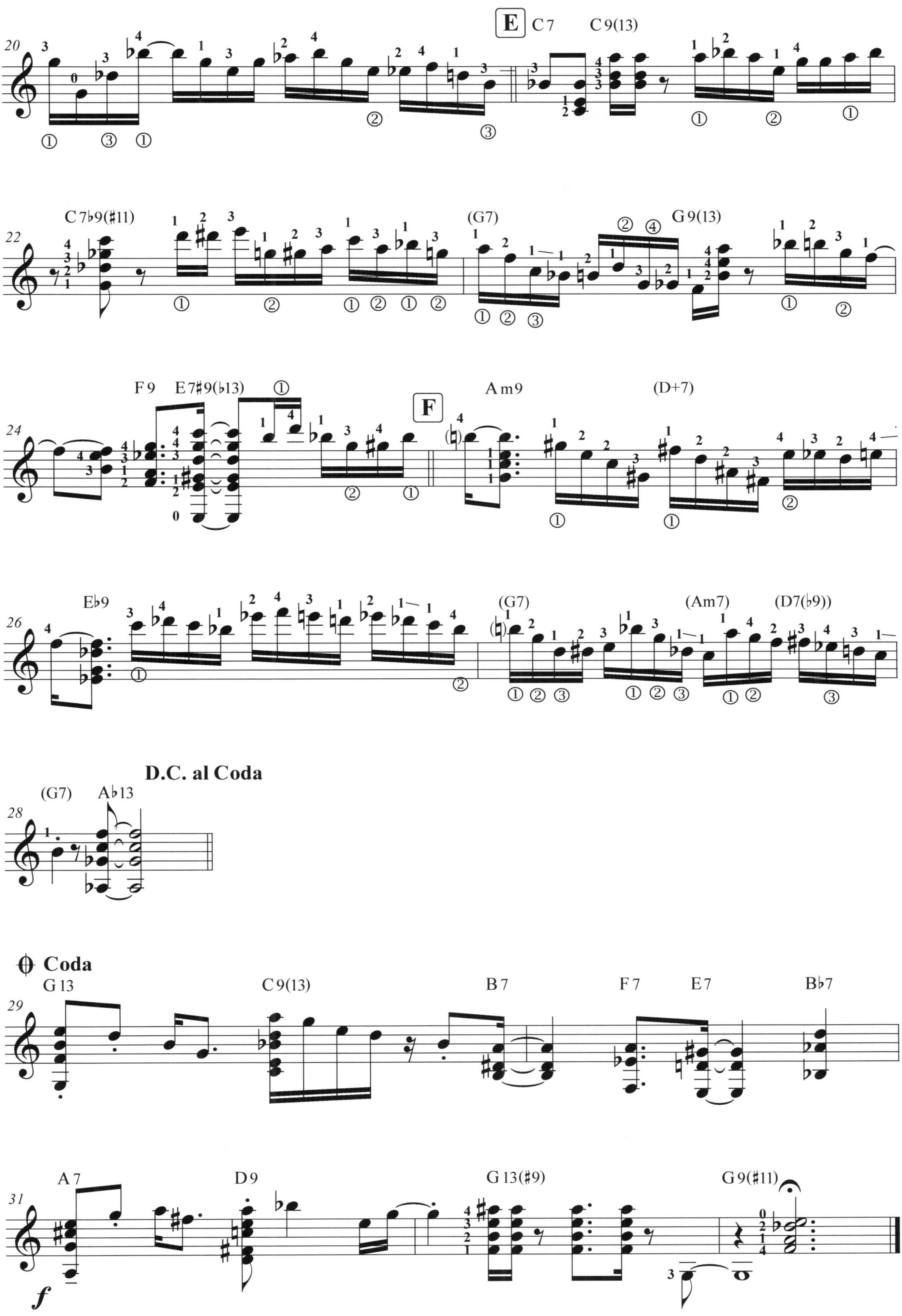
E
C7
C9(13)
C7♭9(♯11)
(G7)
G9(13)
F9
E7♯9(♭13)
F
Am9
(D+7)
E♭9
(G7)
(Am7)
(D7(♭9))
D.C. al Coda
(G7)
A♭13
Coda
G13
C9(13)
B7
F7
E7
B♭7
A7
D9
G13(♯9)
G9(♯11)
f

17

Notes of Winter

Andante (♩ = ca. 70)

Keijo Pennanen

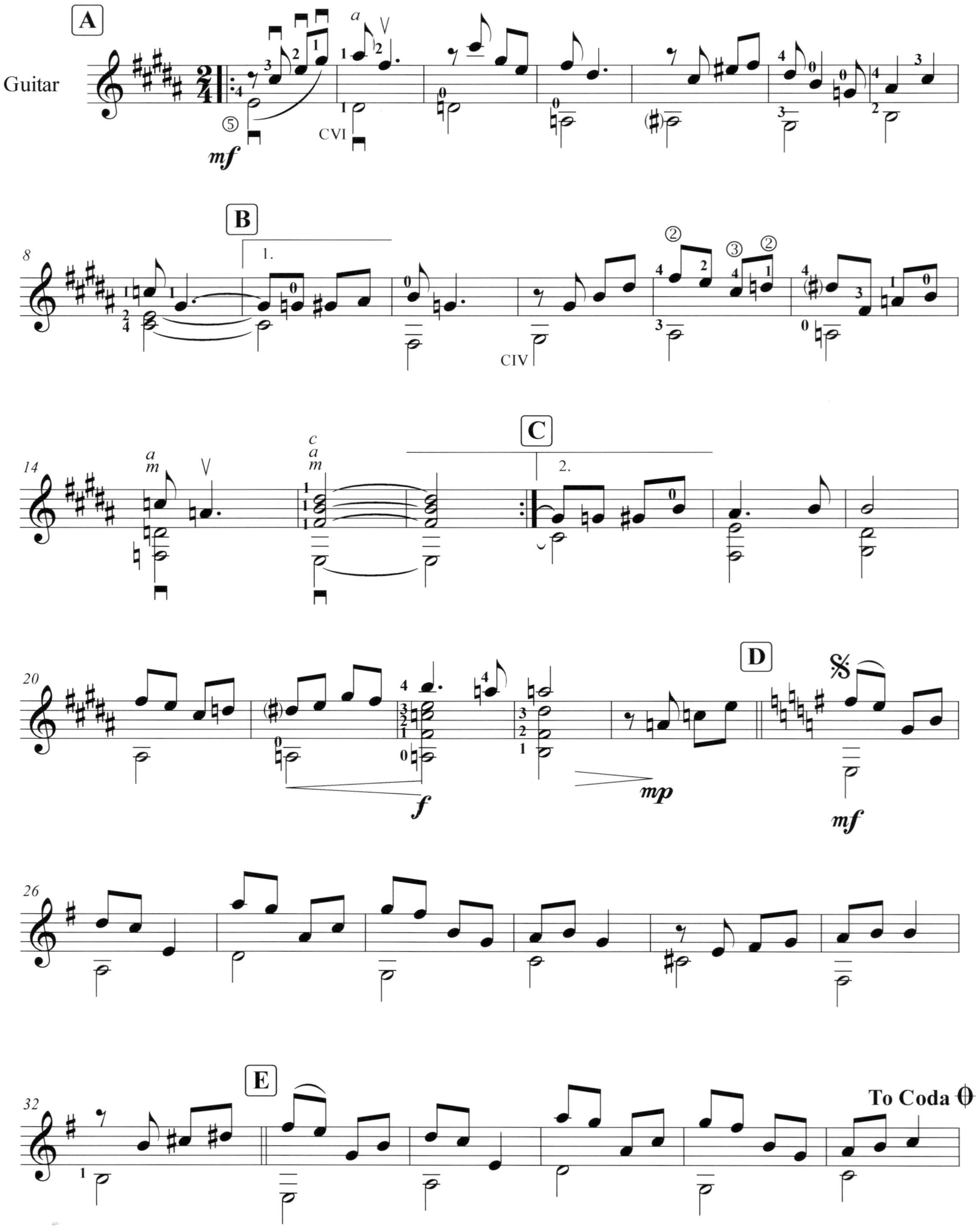

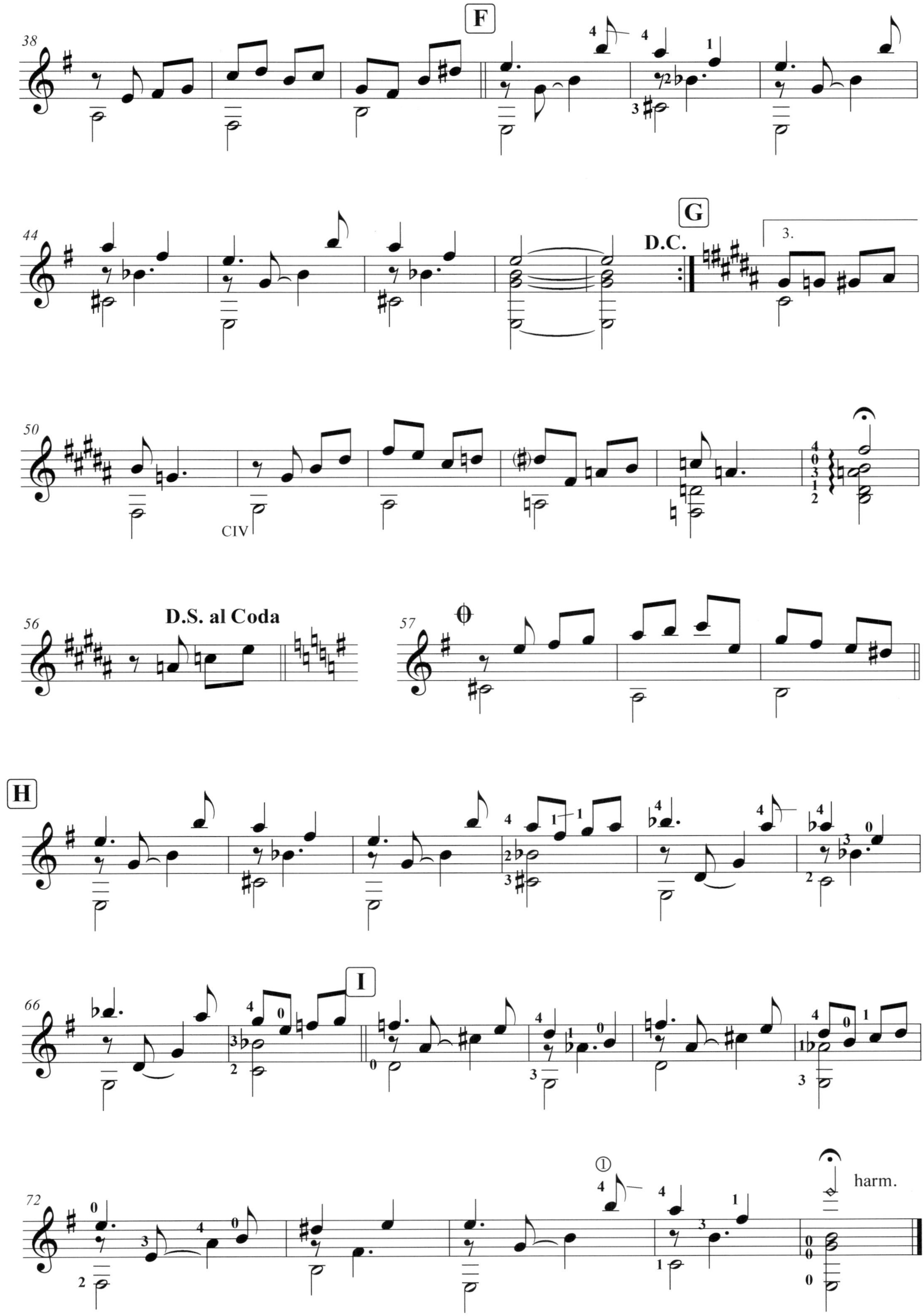
F
G
D.C.
3.
CIV
D.S. al Coda
H
I
harm.

18

Beantown Funk

♩= ca. 105

Keijo Pennanen

x=fret-hand muting.

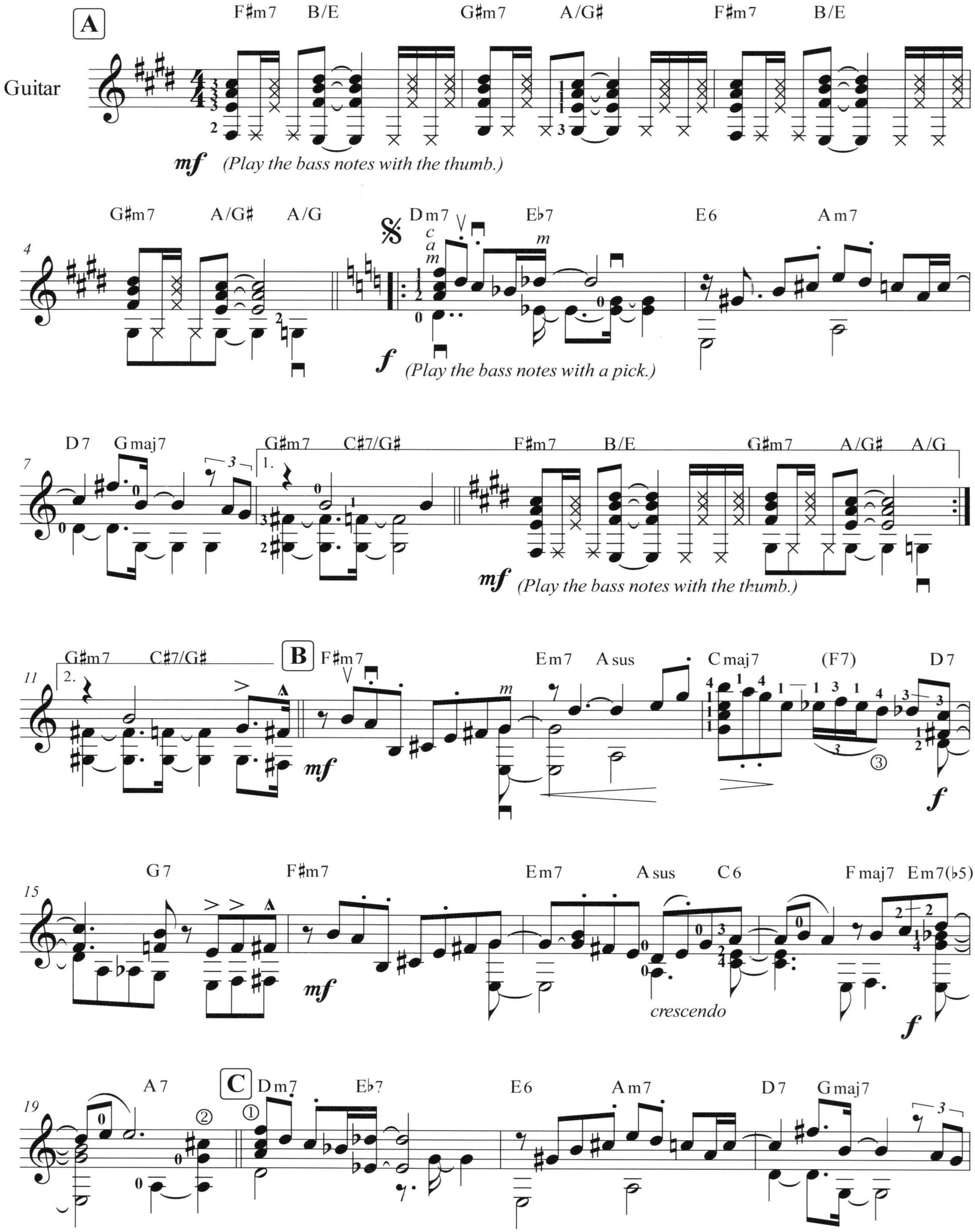

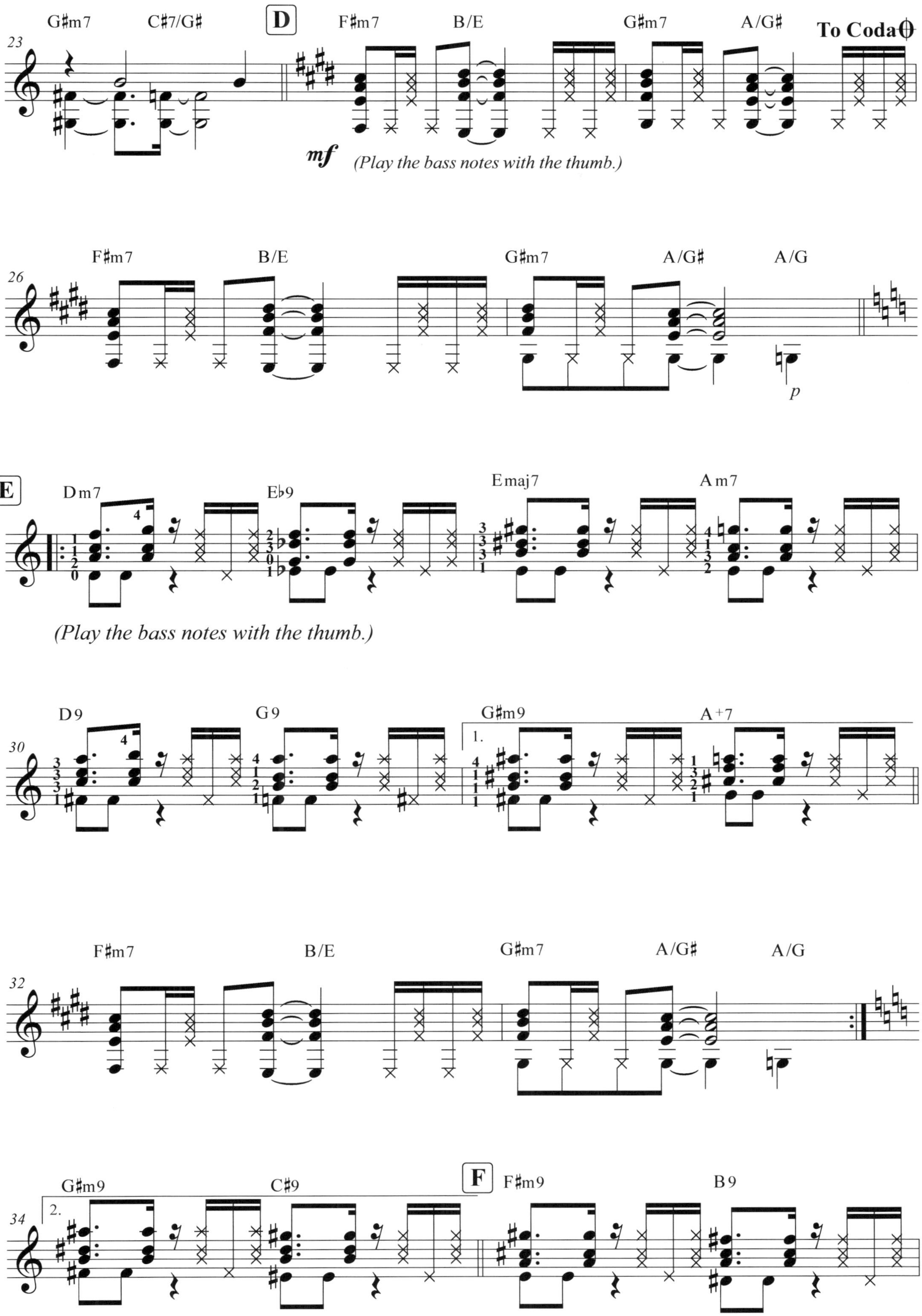
G♯m7 C♯7/G♯
D
F♯m7 B/E G♯m7 A/G♯
To Coda
mf (Play the bass notes with the thumb.)
F♯m7 B/E G♯m7 A/G♯ A/G
p
E
Dm7 E♭9 Emaj7 Am7
(Play the bass notes with the thumb.)
D9 G9 G♯m9 A+7
1.
F♯m7 B/E G♯m7 A/G♯ A/G
G♯m9 C♯9
2.
F
F♯m9 B9

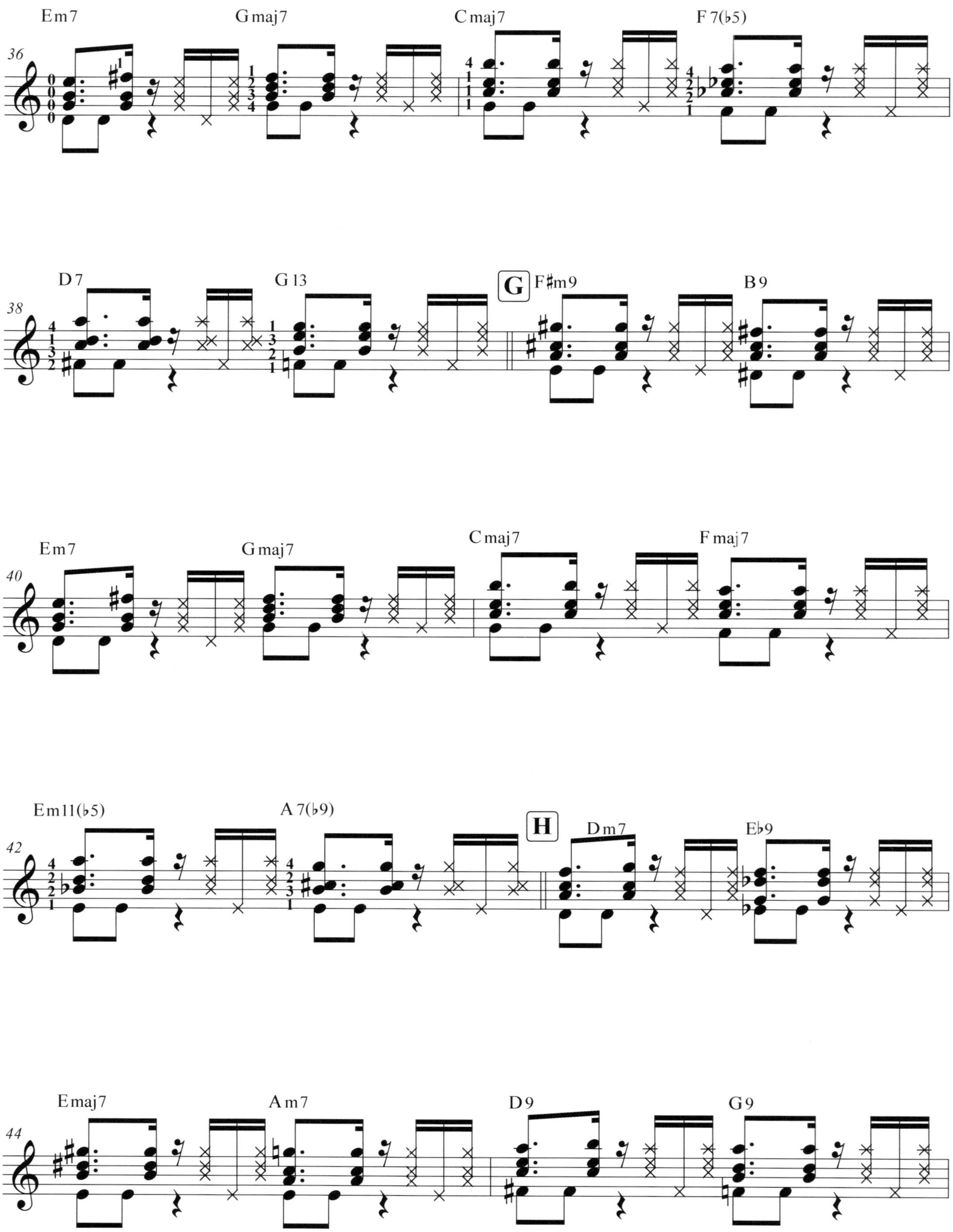
Em7
Gmaj7
Cmaj7
F7(♭5)
D7
G13
G
F♯m9
B9
Em7
Gmaj7
Cmaj7
Fmaj7
Em11(♭5)
A7(♭9)
H
Dm7
E♭9
Emaj7
Am7
D9
G9

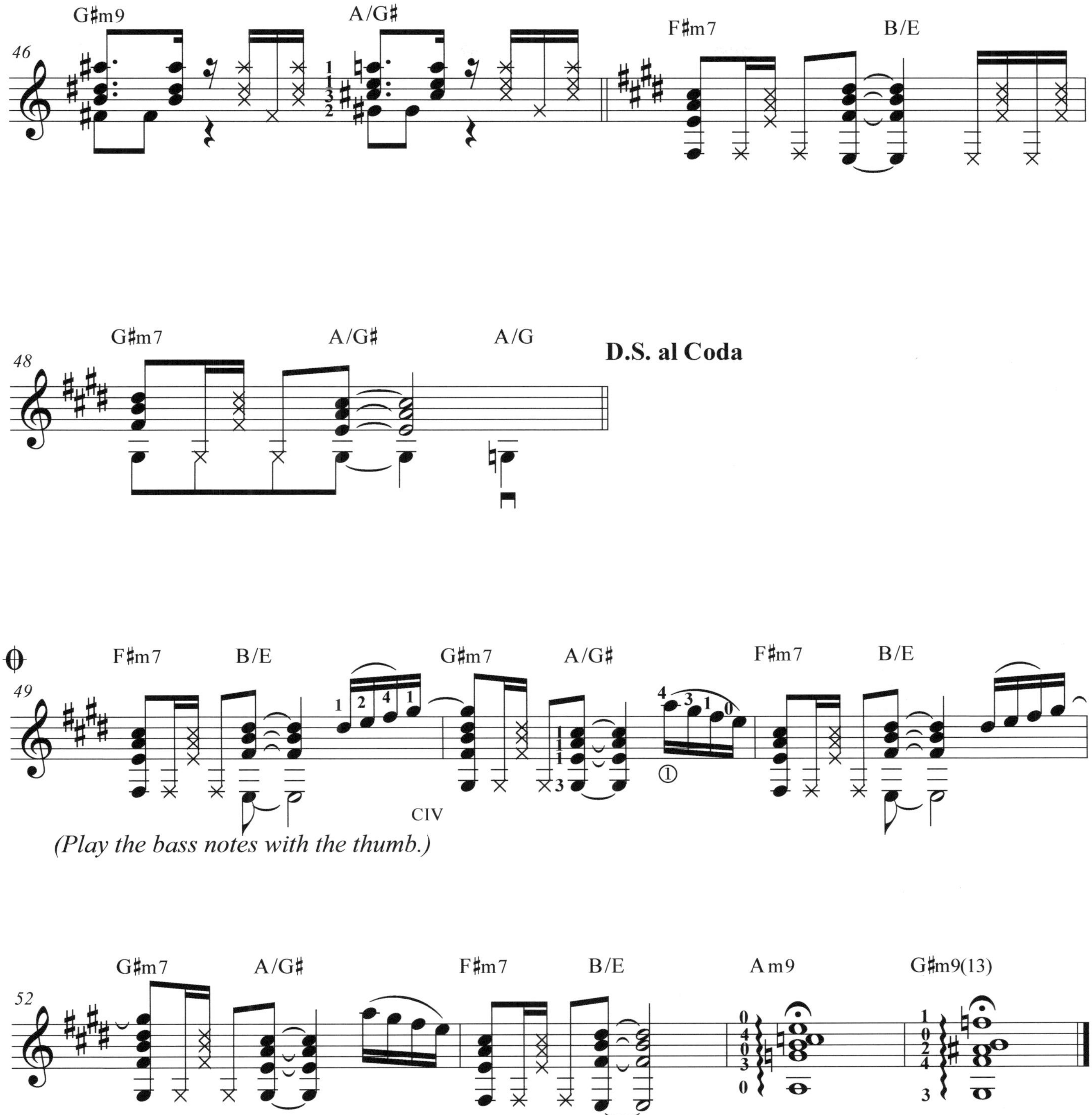
G♯m9
A/G♯
F♯m7
B/E
G♯m7
A/G♯
A/G
D.S. al Coda
F♯m7
B/E
G♯m7
A/G♯
F♯m7
B/E
CIV
(Play the bass notes with the thumb.)
G♯m7
A/G♯
F♯m7
B/E
Am9
G♯m9(13)

19

Toward Home

Allegro (♩ = ca. 120)

Keijo Pennanen

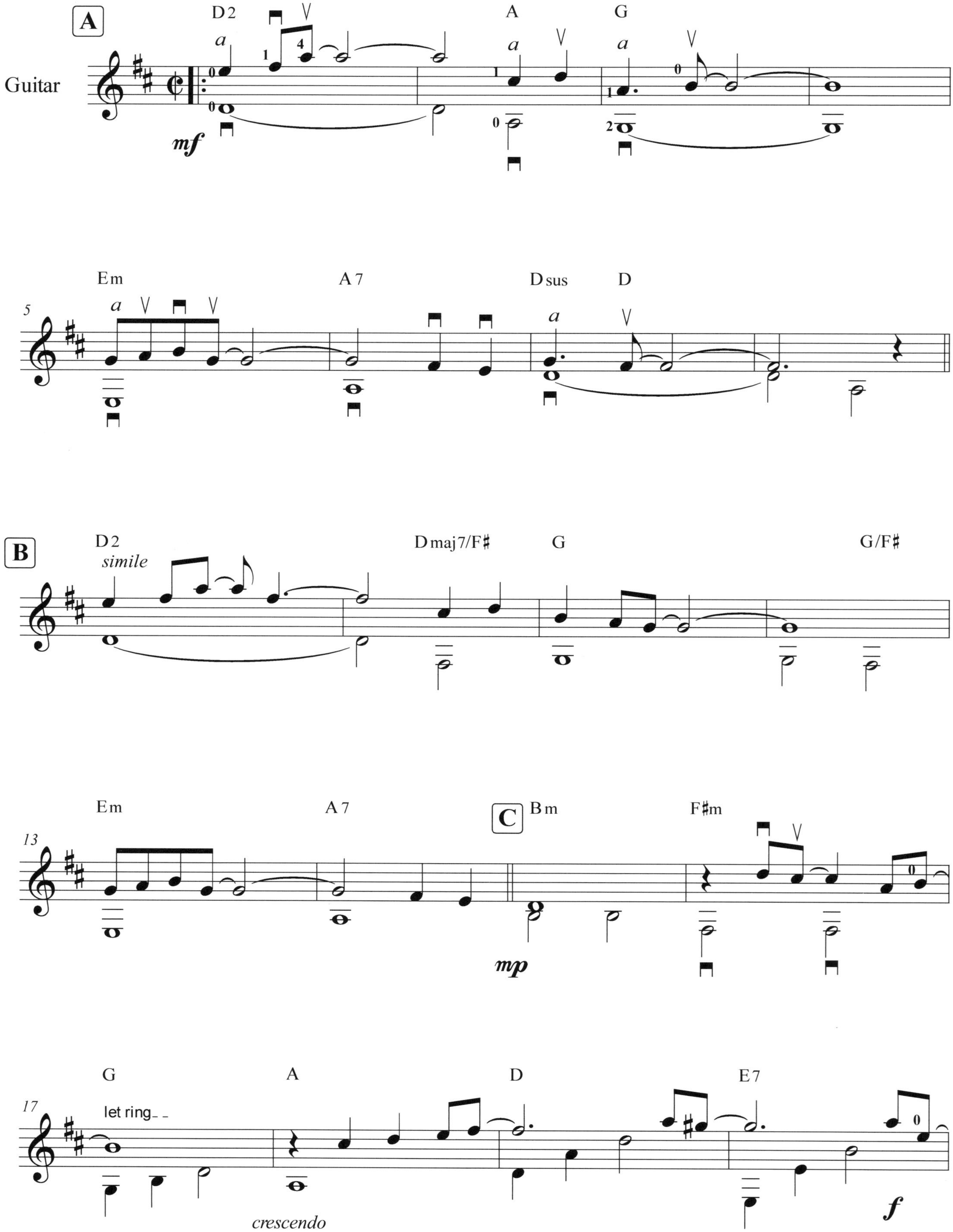

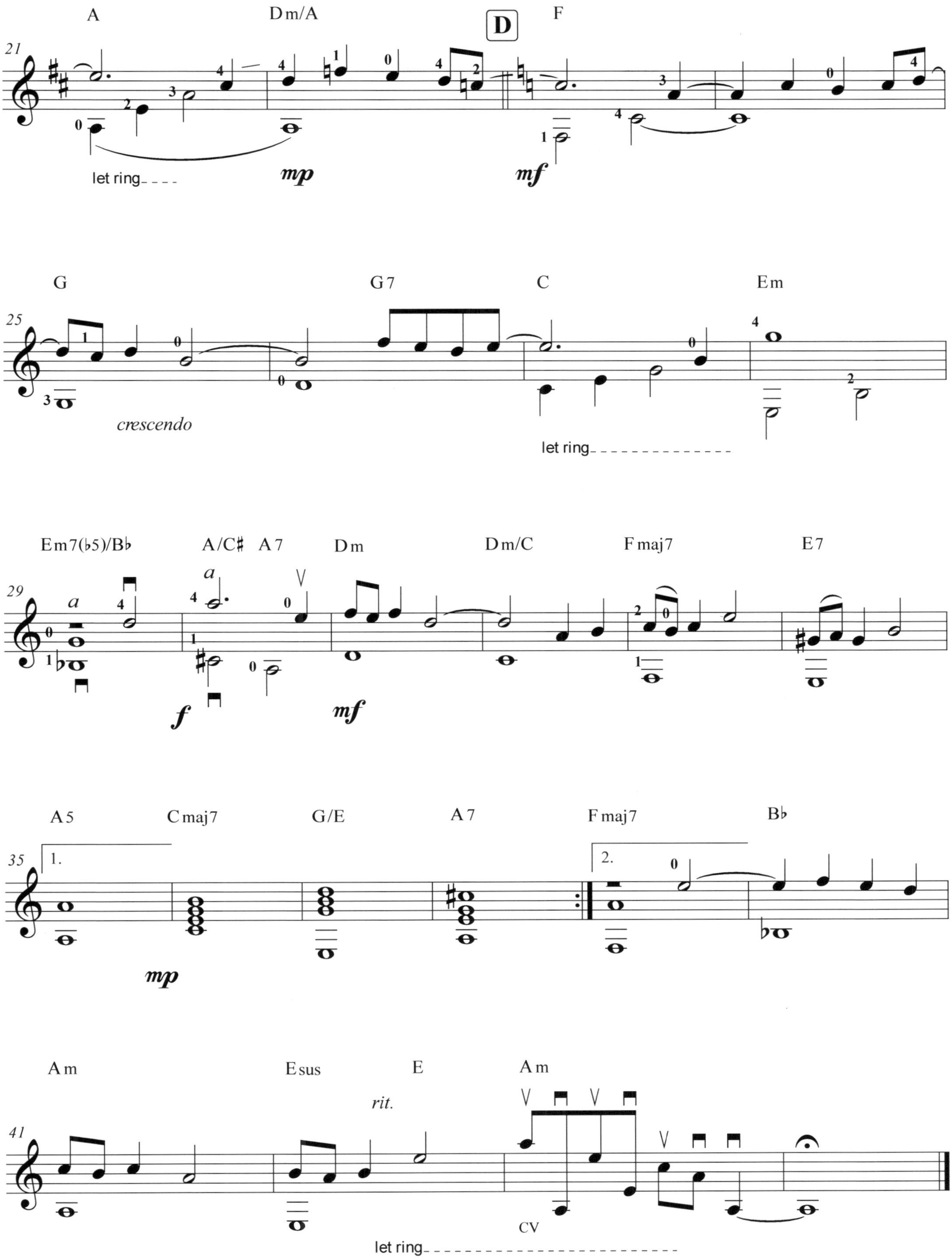
A
Dm/A
D
F
let ring
mp
mf
G
G7
C
Em
crescendo
let ring
Em7(♭5)/B♭
A/C♯
A7
Dm
Dm/C
Fmaj7
E7
f
mf
A5
Cmaj7
G/E
A7
Fmaj7
B♭
1.
2.
mp
Am
Esus
E
Am
rit.
CV
let ring

20

Samba Shoreline

♩ = ca. 80

Keijo Pennanen

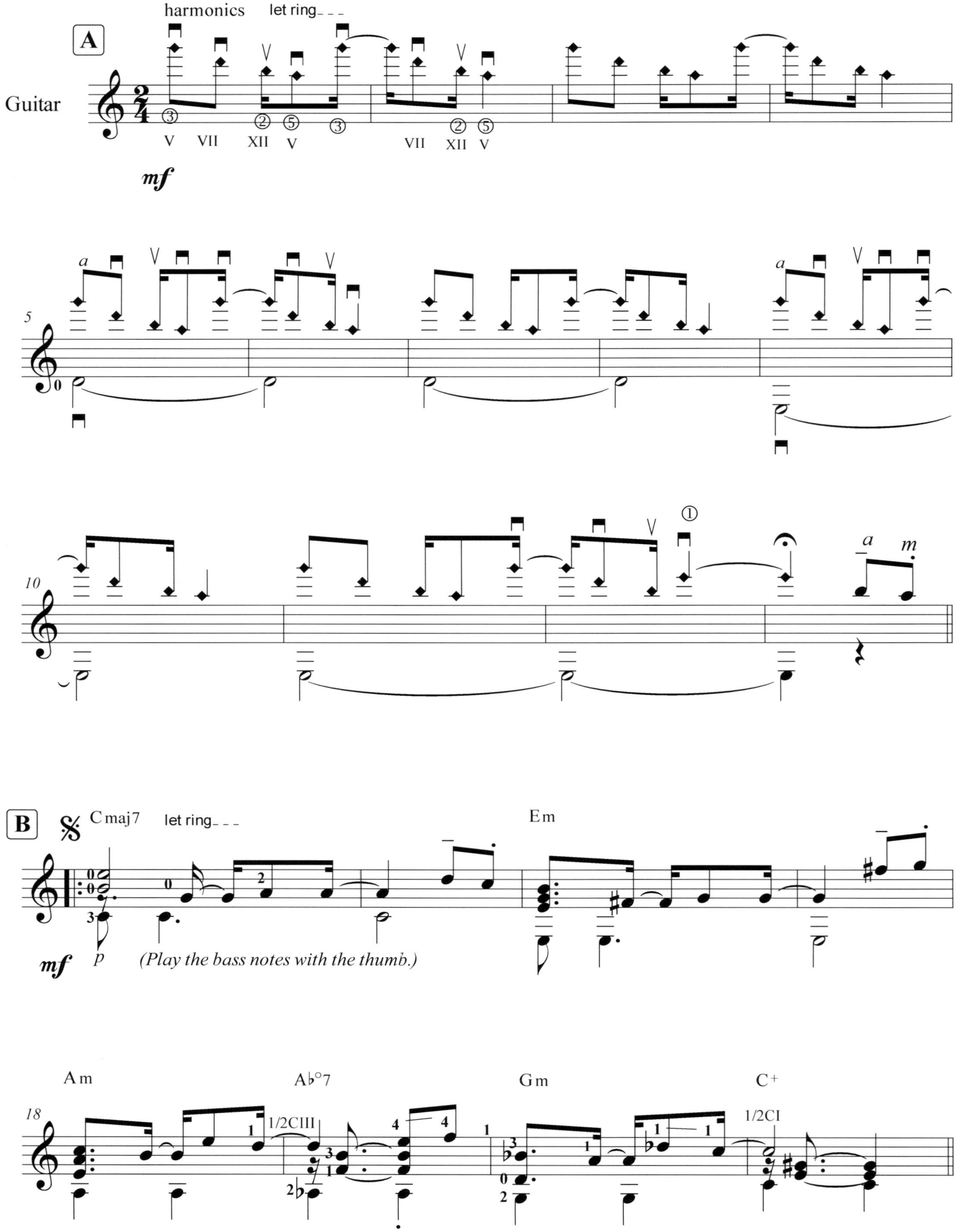

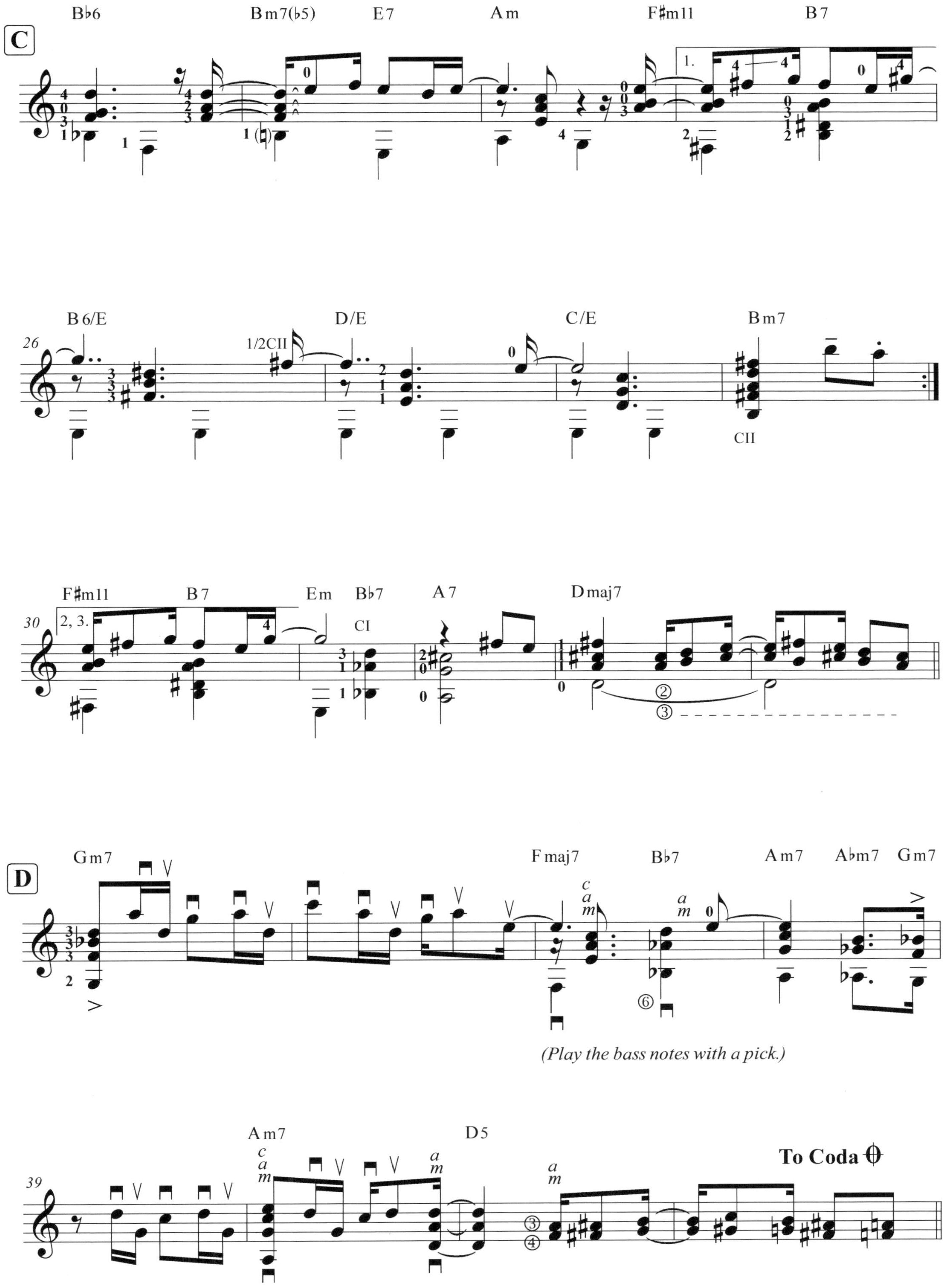
C
B♭6
Bm7(♭5)
E7
Am
F♯m11
B7
1.
26
B6/E
1/2CII
D/E
C/E
Bm7
CII
30
F♯m11
B7
2, 3.
Em
B♭7
CI
A7
Dmaj7
D
Gm7
Fmaj7
B♭7
Am7
A♭m7
Gm7
(Play the bass notes with a pick.)
39
Am7
D5
To Coda

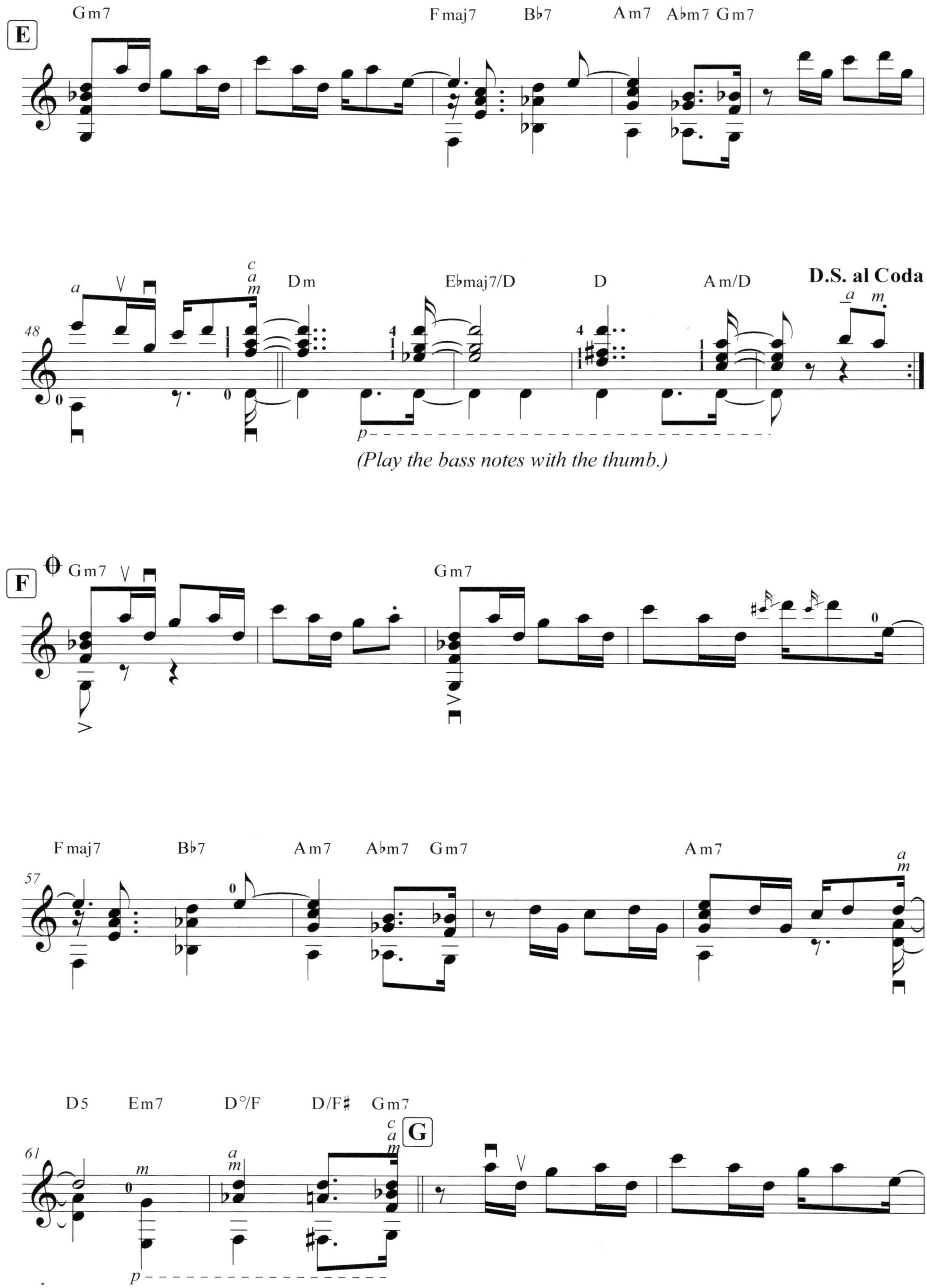
E
Gm7
Fmaj7
B♭7
Am7
A♭m7
Gm7
48
Dm
E♭maj7/D
D
Am/D
D.S. al Coda
(Play the bass notes with the thumb.)
F
Gm7
Gm7
57
Fmaj7
B♭7
Am7
A♭m7
Gm7
Am7
61
D5
Em7
D°/F
D/F♯
Gm7
G

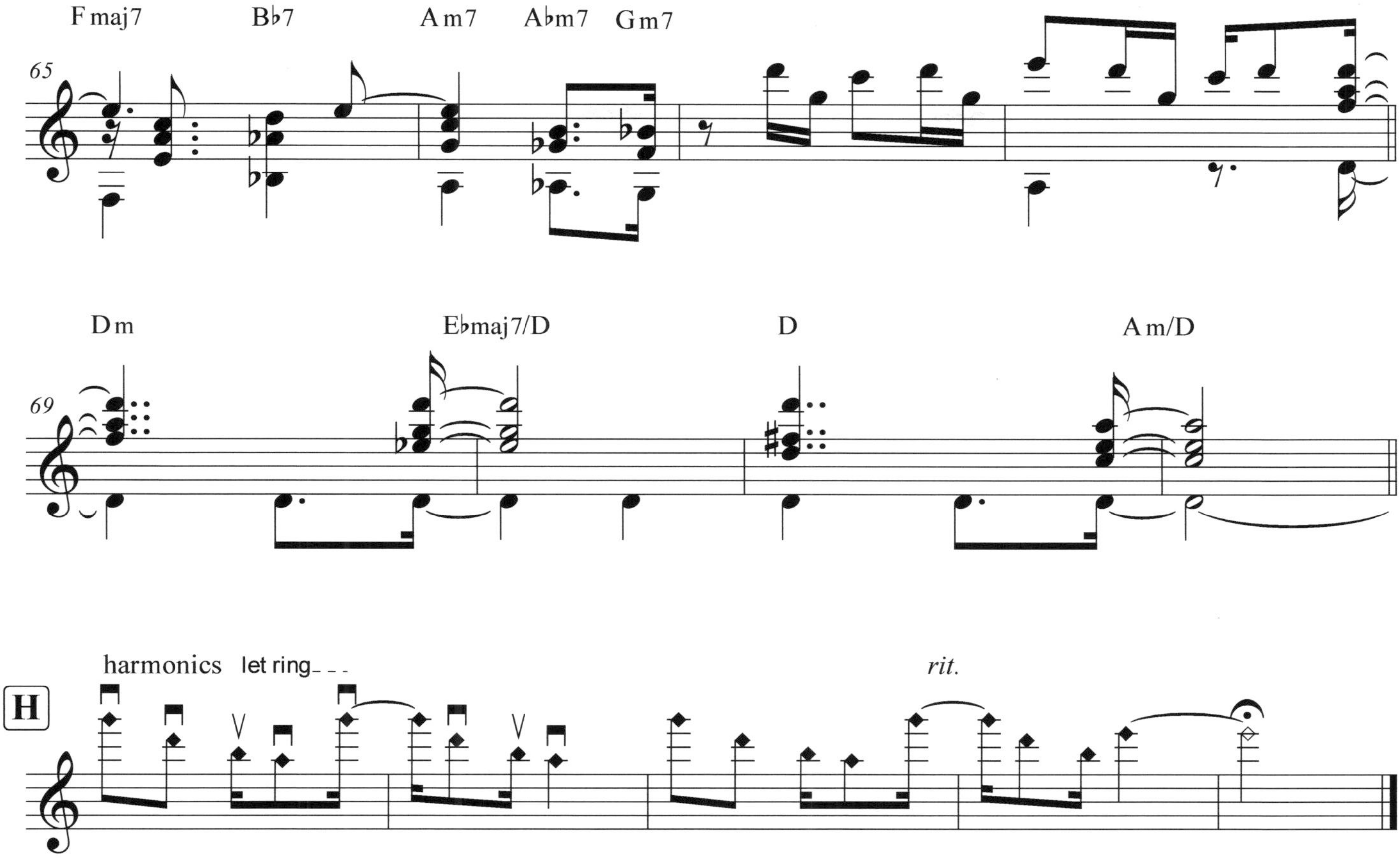
65
Fmaj7
B♭7
Am7
A♭m7
Gm7
69
Dm
E♭maj7/D
D
Am/D
H
harmonics let ring
rit.

21

Portrait of a Memory

Andante (♩ = ca. 76)

Keijo Pennanen

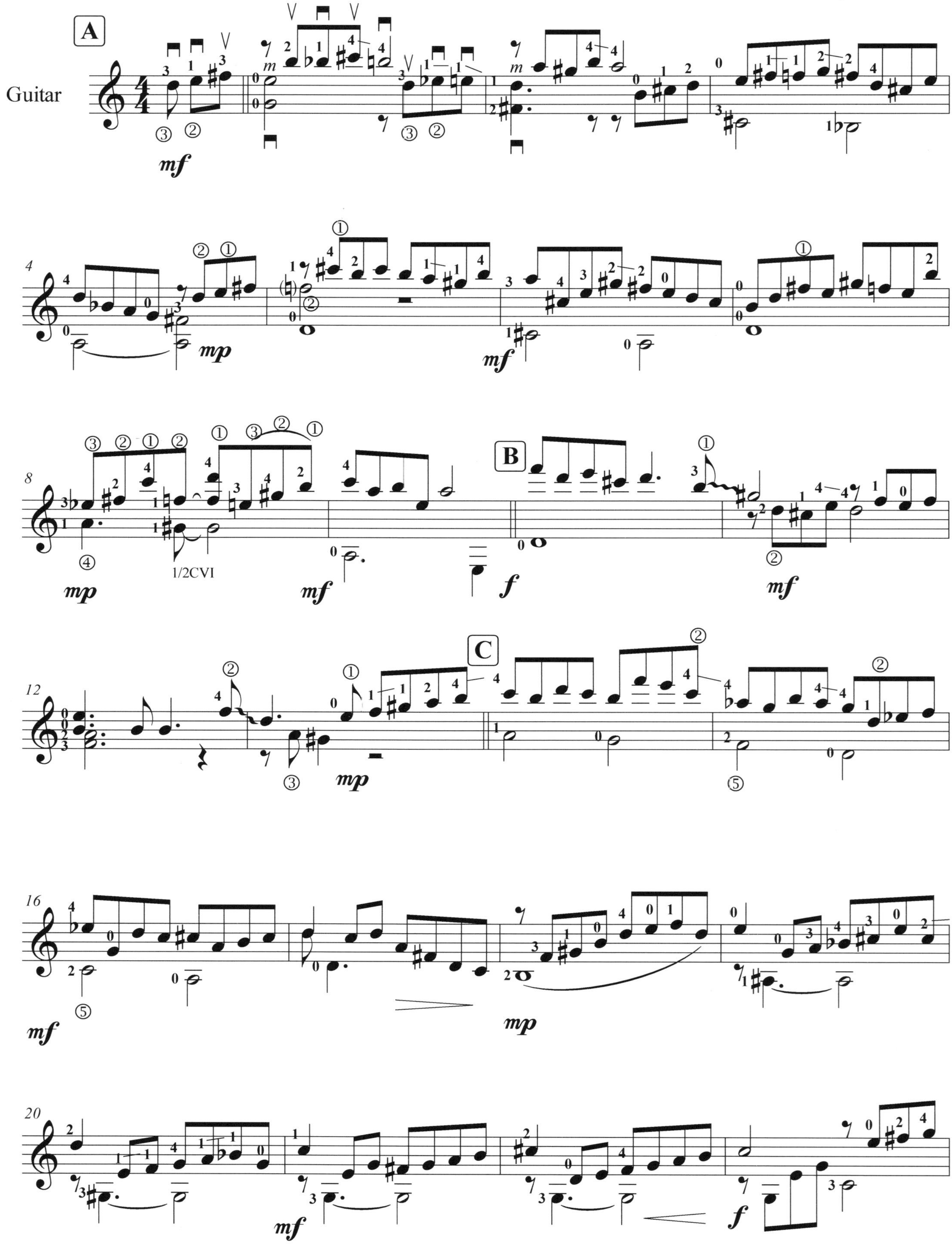

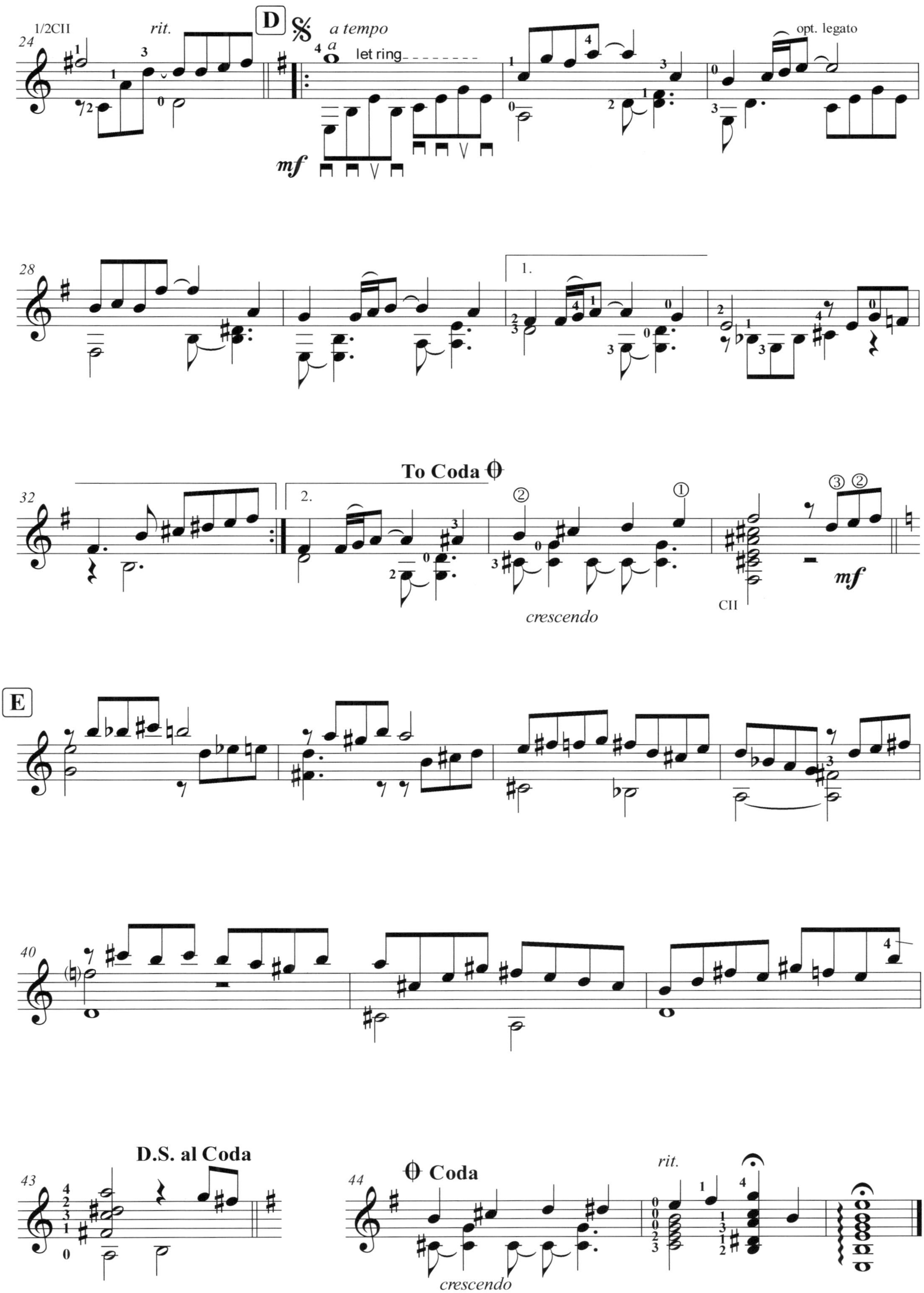
1/2CII
rit.
D
a tempo
let ring
mf
opt. legato
1.
2.
To Coda
crescendo
CII
mf
E
D.S. al Coda
Coda
rit.
crescendo

22

Cielo Nocturno

♩. = ca. 54

Keijo Pennanen

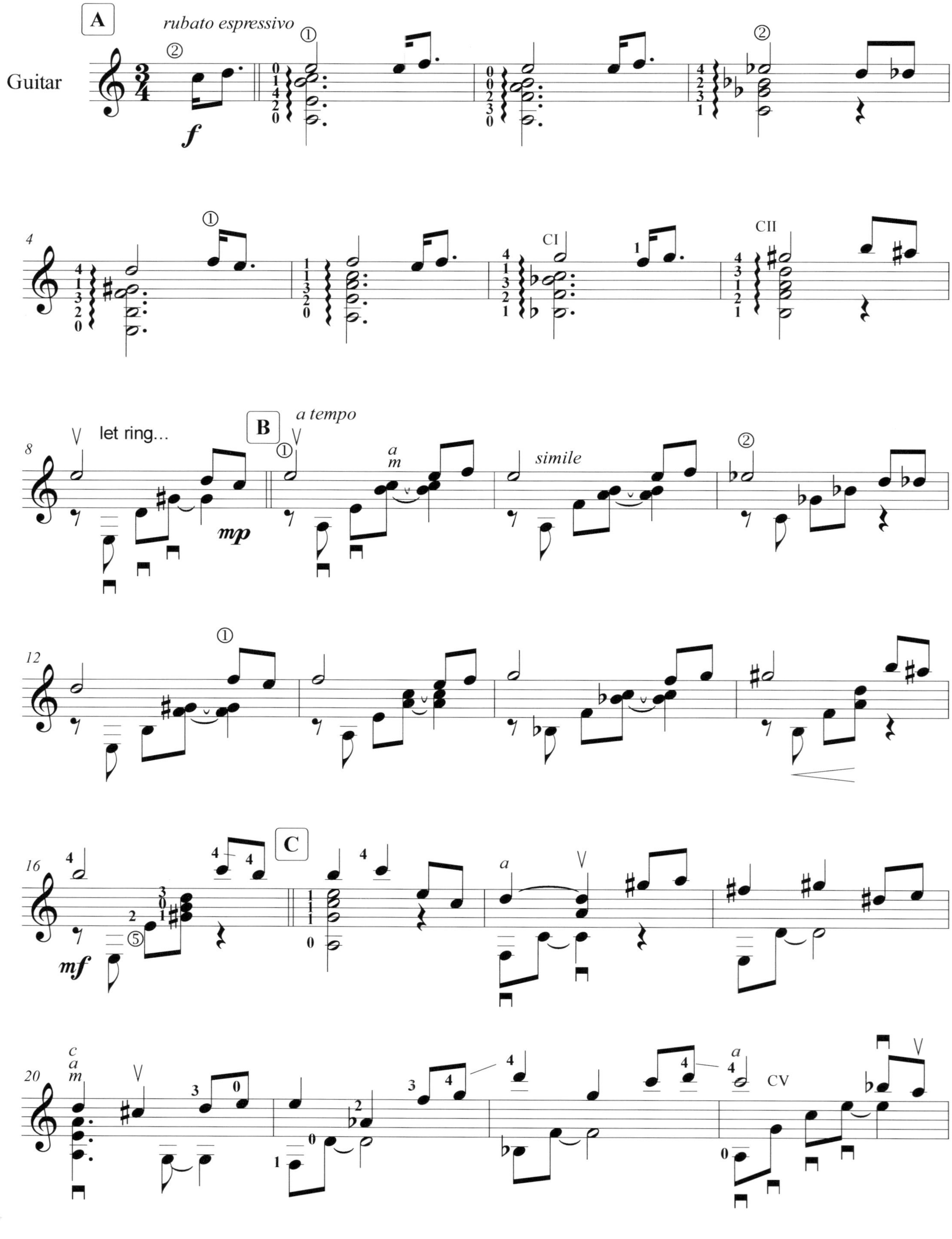

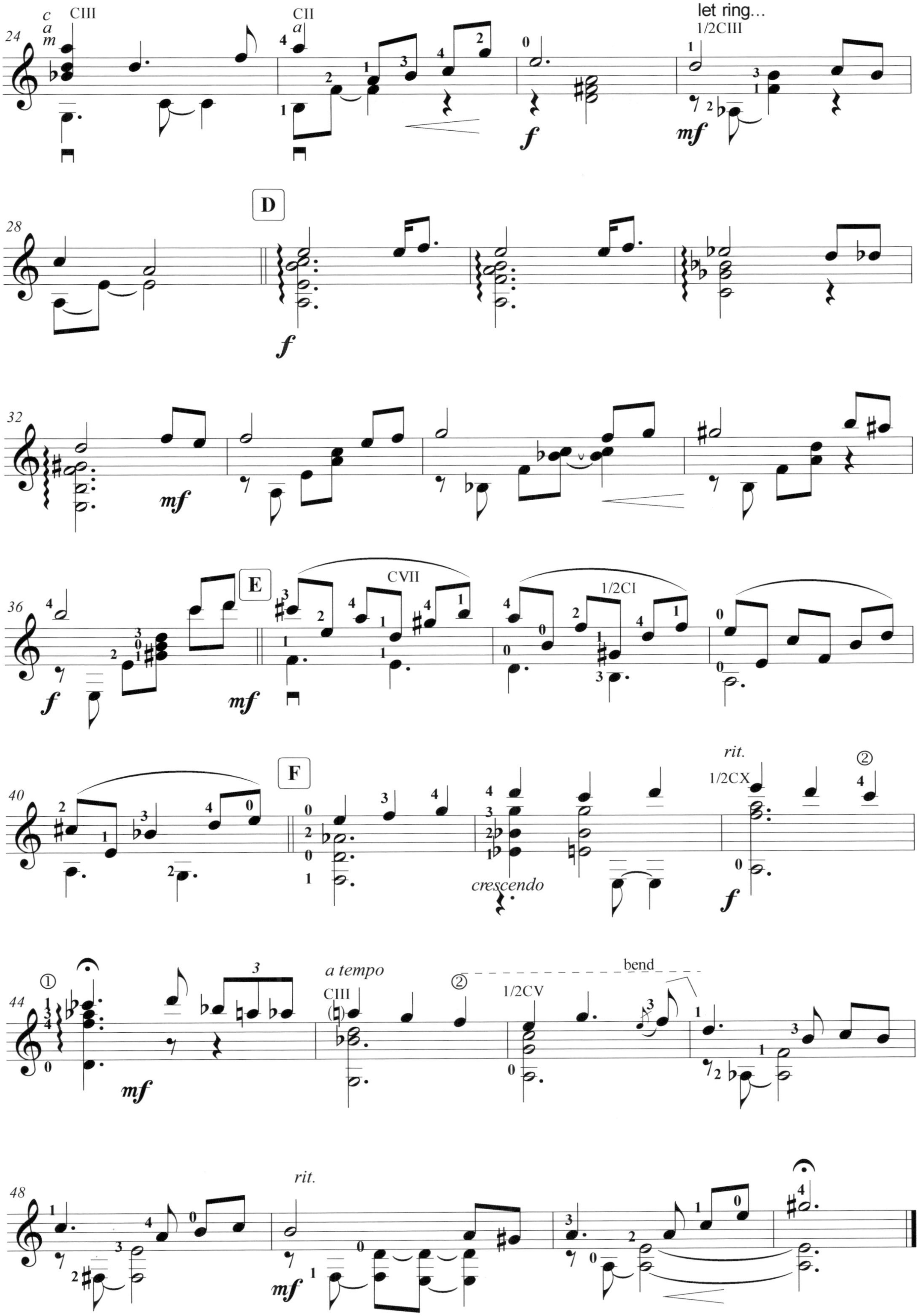
CIII
CII
let ring...
1/2CIII
D
E
CVII
1/2CI
F
rit.
1/2CX
crescendo
a tempo
CIII
bend
1/2CV
rit.

Twelfth Moment

(A Twelve-Tone Row)

Rubato

Keijo Pennanen

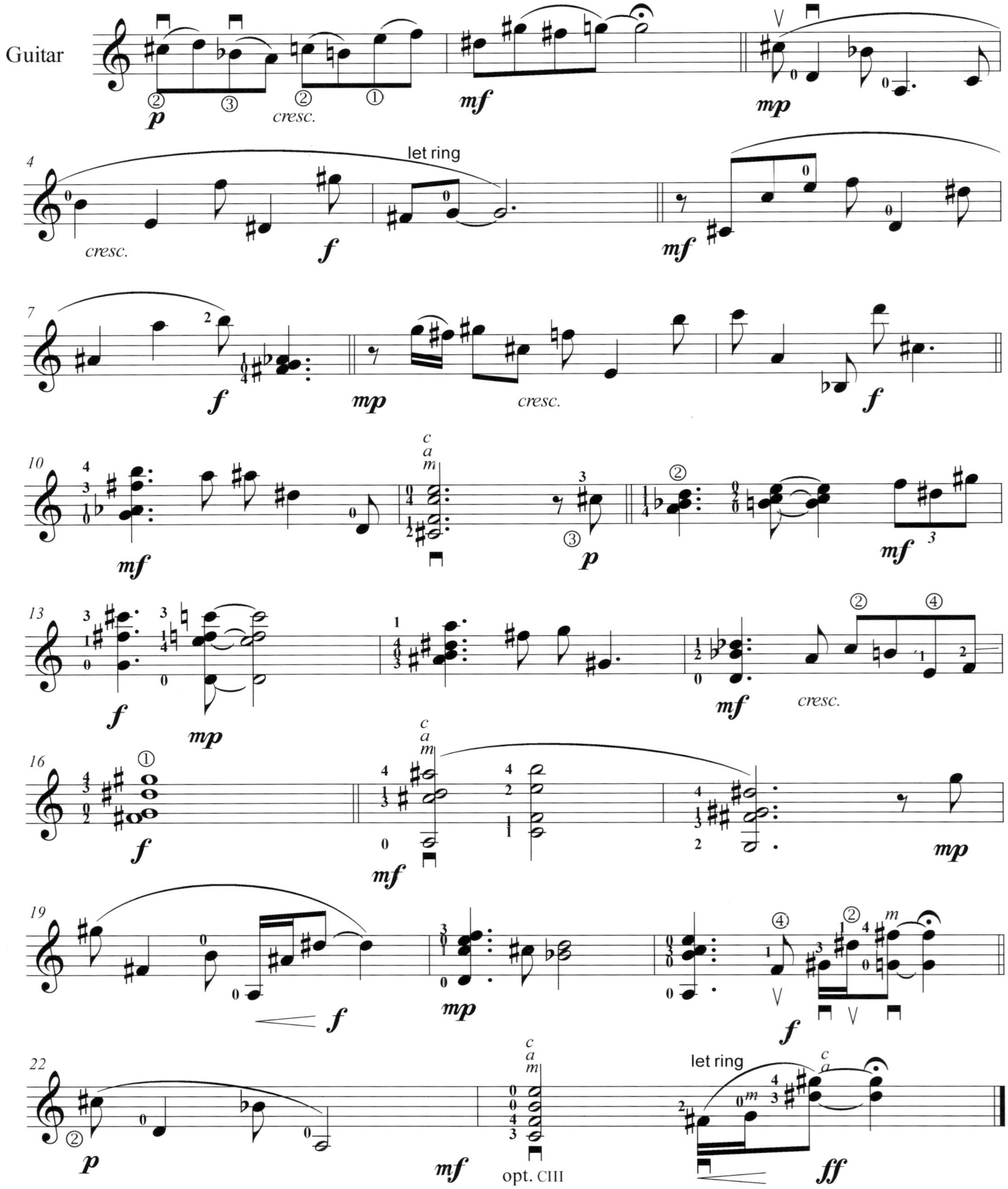

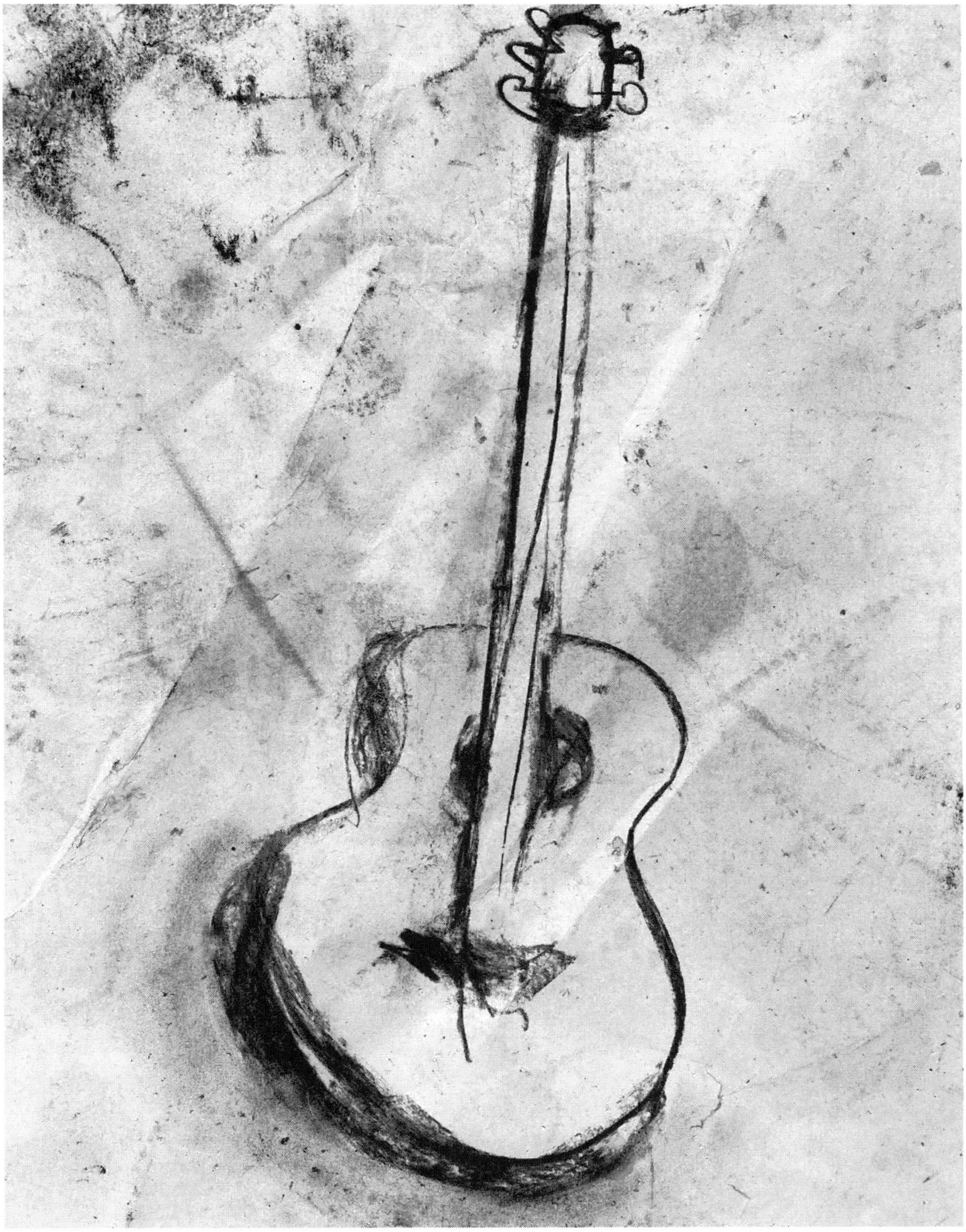

Drawing by Erno Pennanen

A New Frontier

Allegro (♩ = ca. 120)

Dropped-D Tuning

Keijo Pennanen

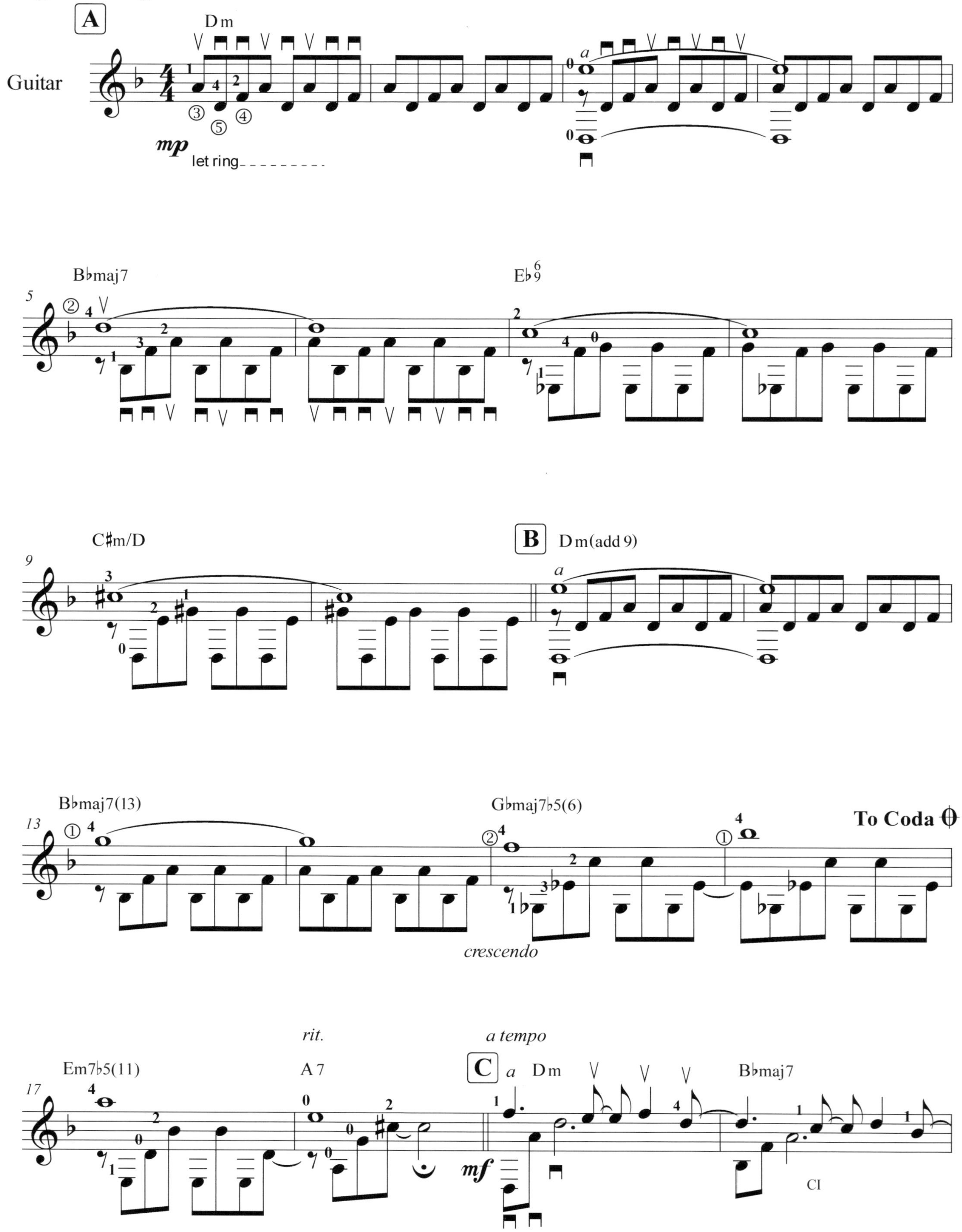

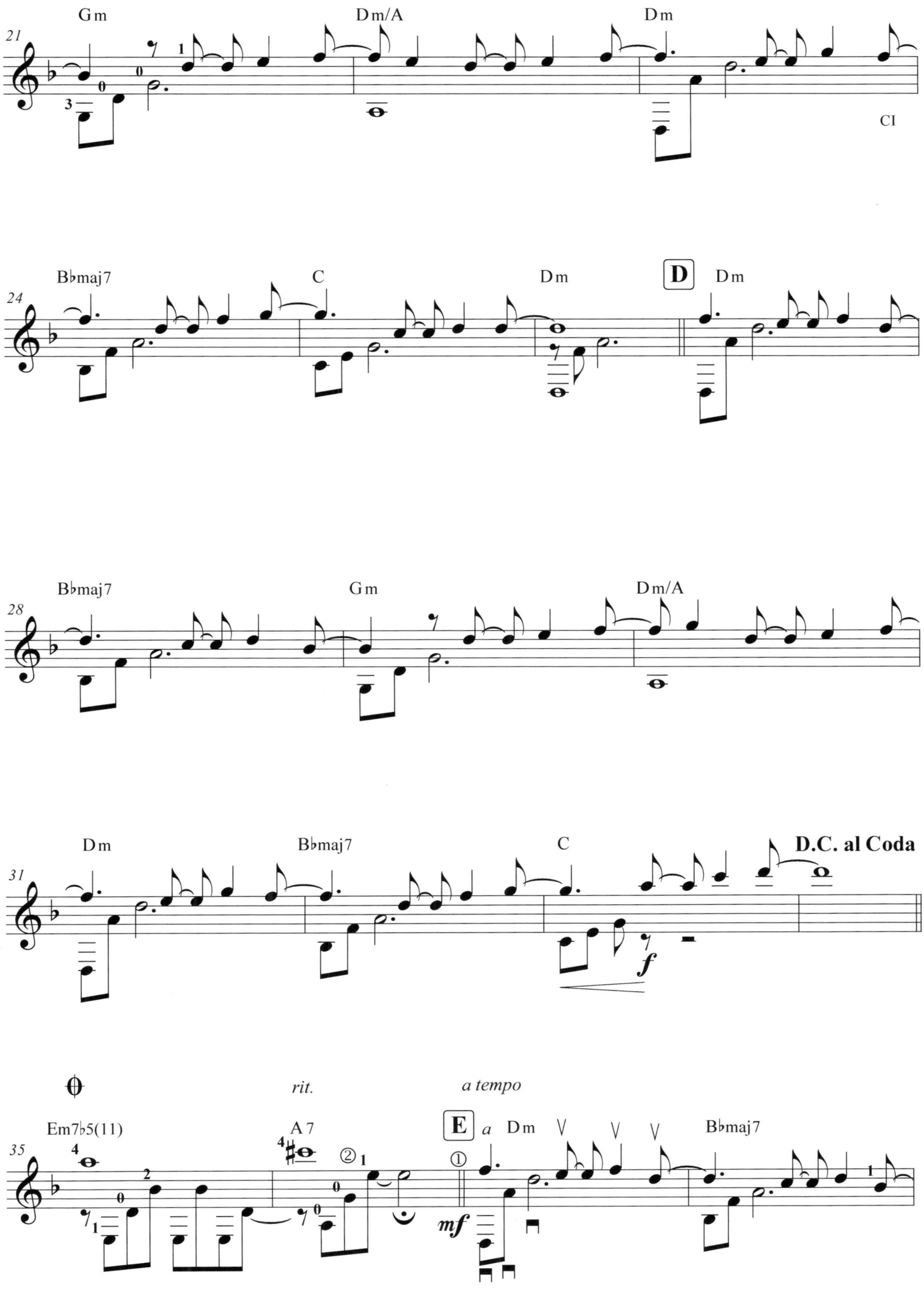

Gm
Dm/A
Dm
CI
Bbmaj7
C
Dm
D
Dm
Bbmaj7
Gm
Dm/A
Dm
Bbmaj7
C
D.C. al Coda
rit.
a tempo
Em7b5(11)
A7
E
a
Dm
Bbmaj7
mf
f

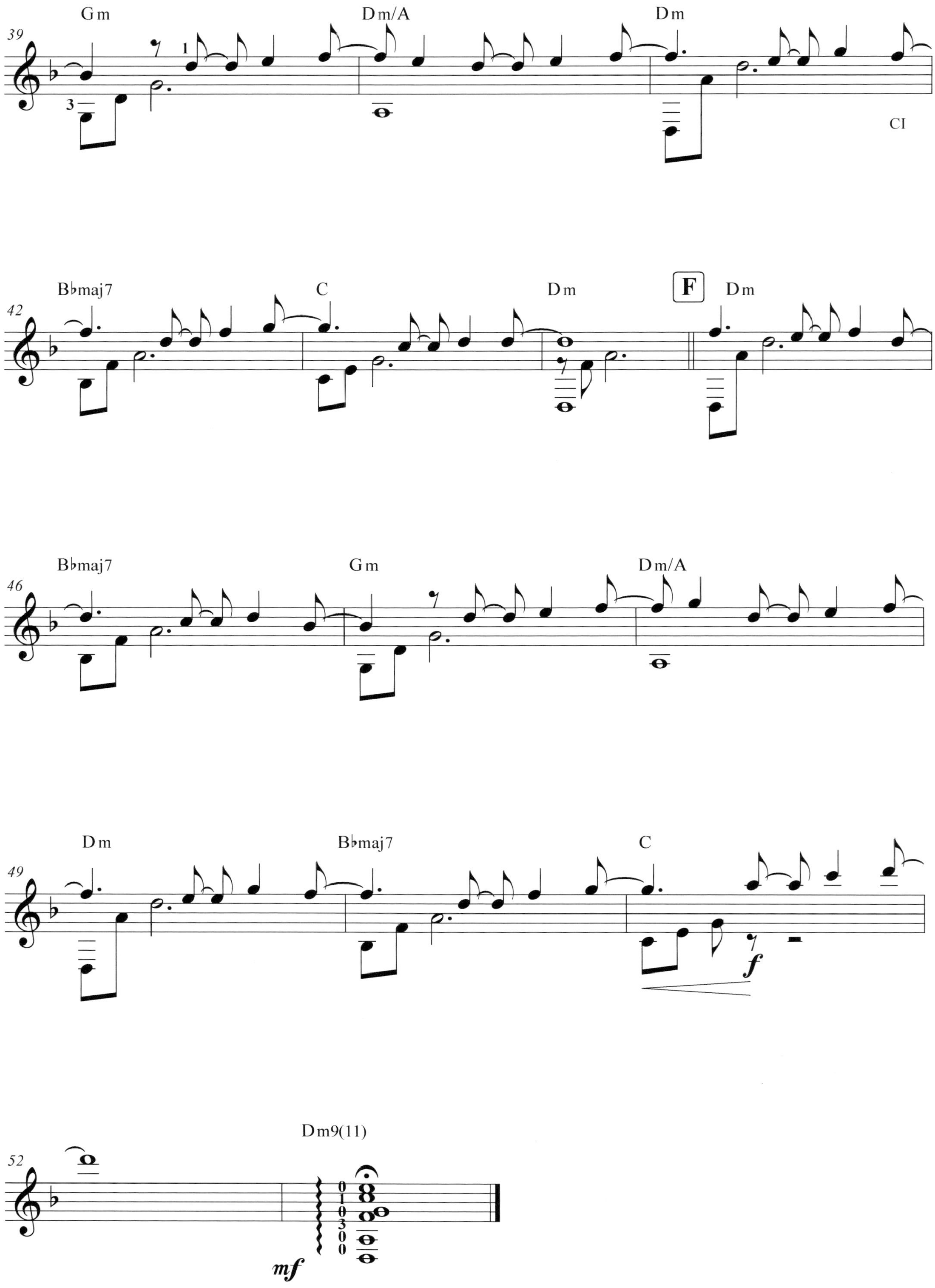

Gm
D m/A
D m
CI
B♭maj7
C
D m
F
D m
B♭maj7
Gm
D m/A
D m
B♭maj7
C
f
Dm9(11)
mf

25

Un Poco de Flamenco

Andante (♩ = ca. 92)

Keijo Pennanen

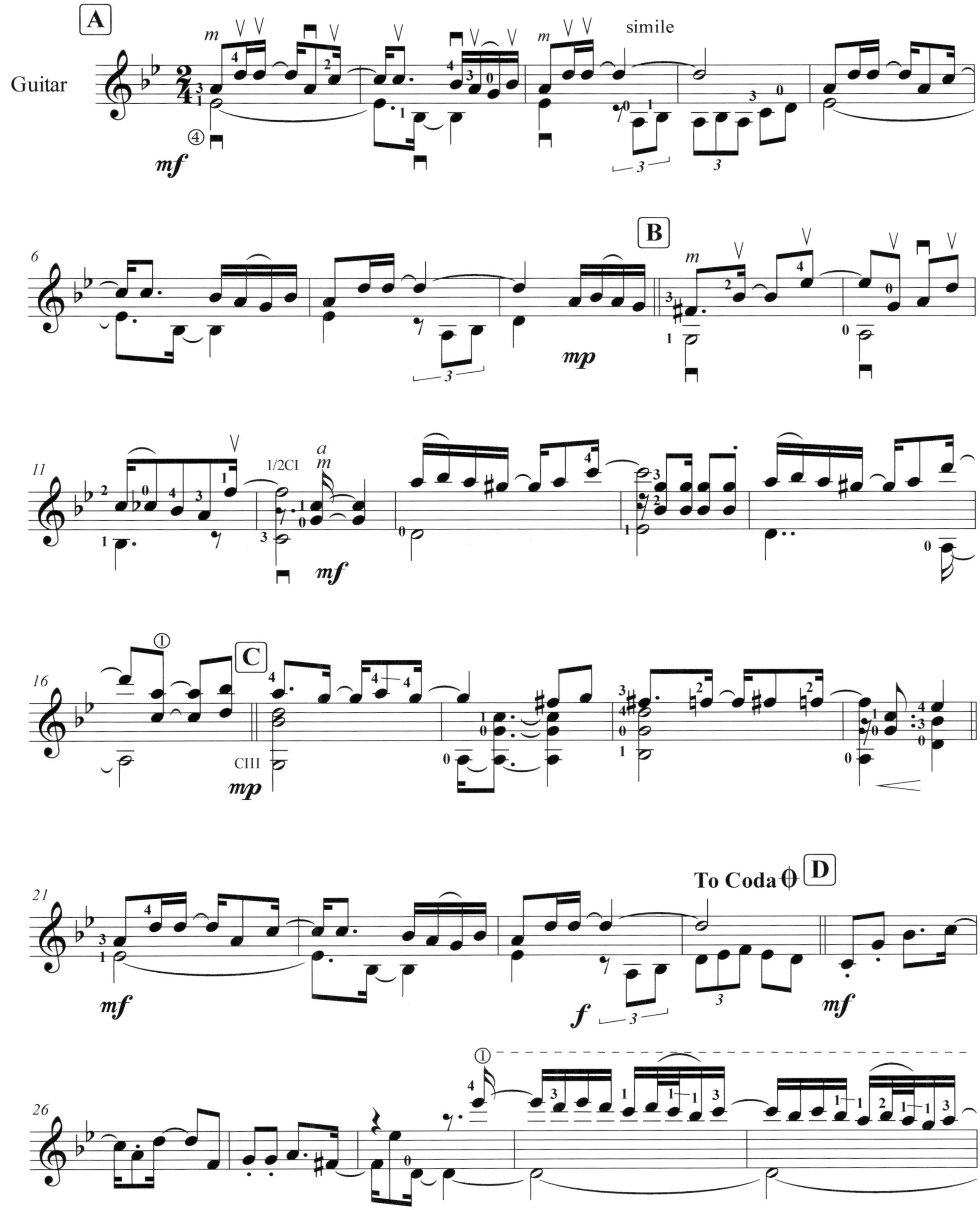

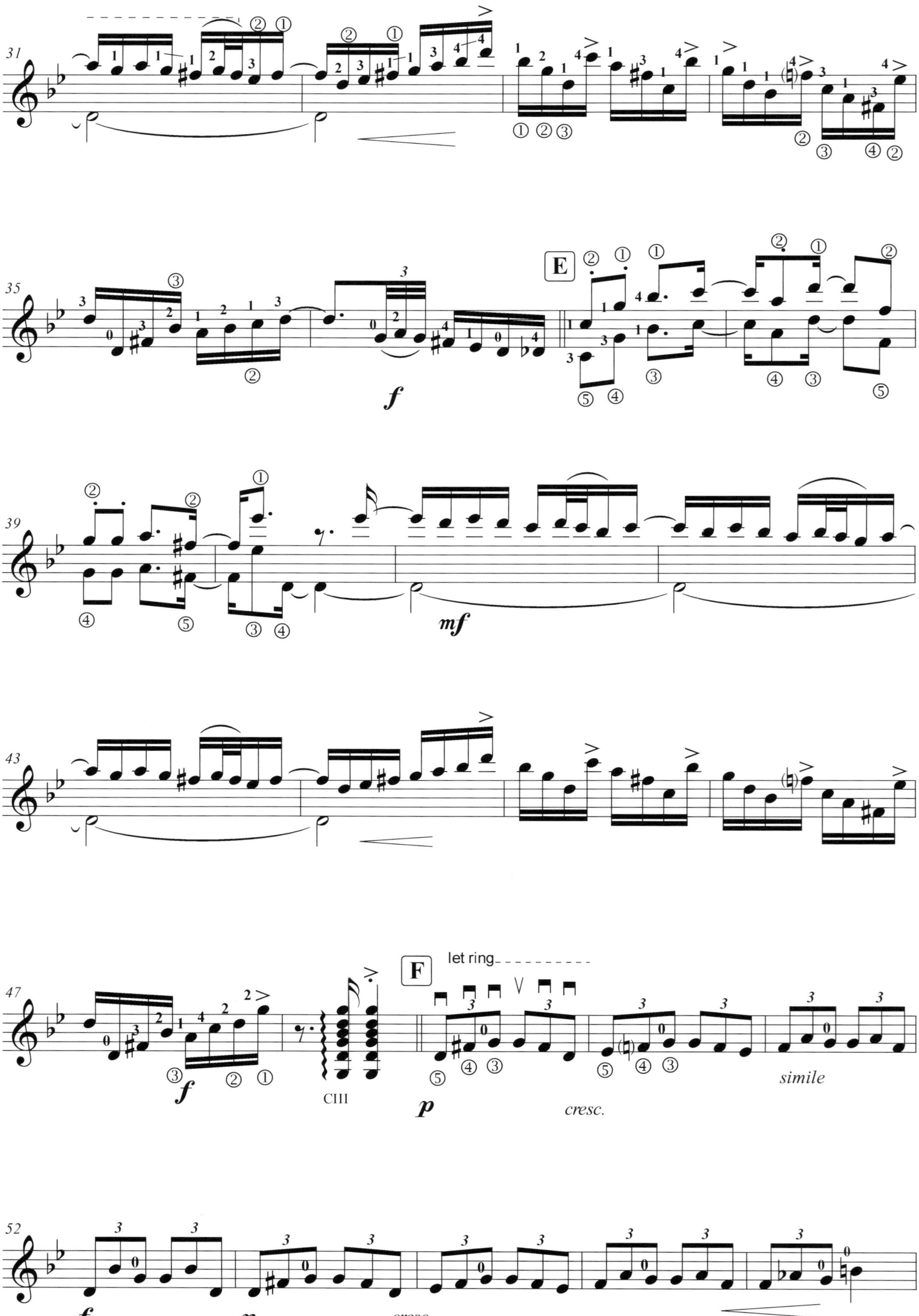
E
F
let ring
simile
cresc.
CIII
cresc.

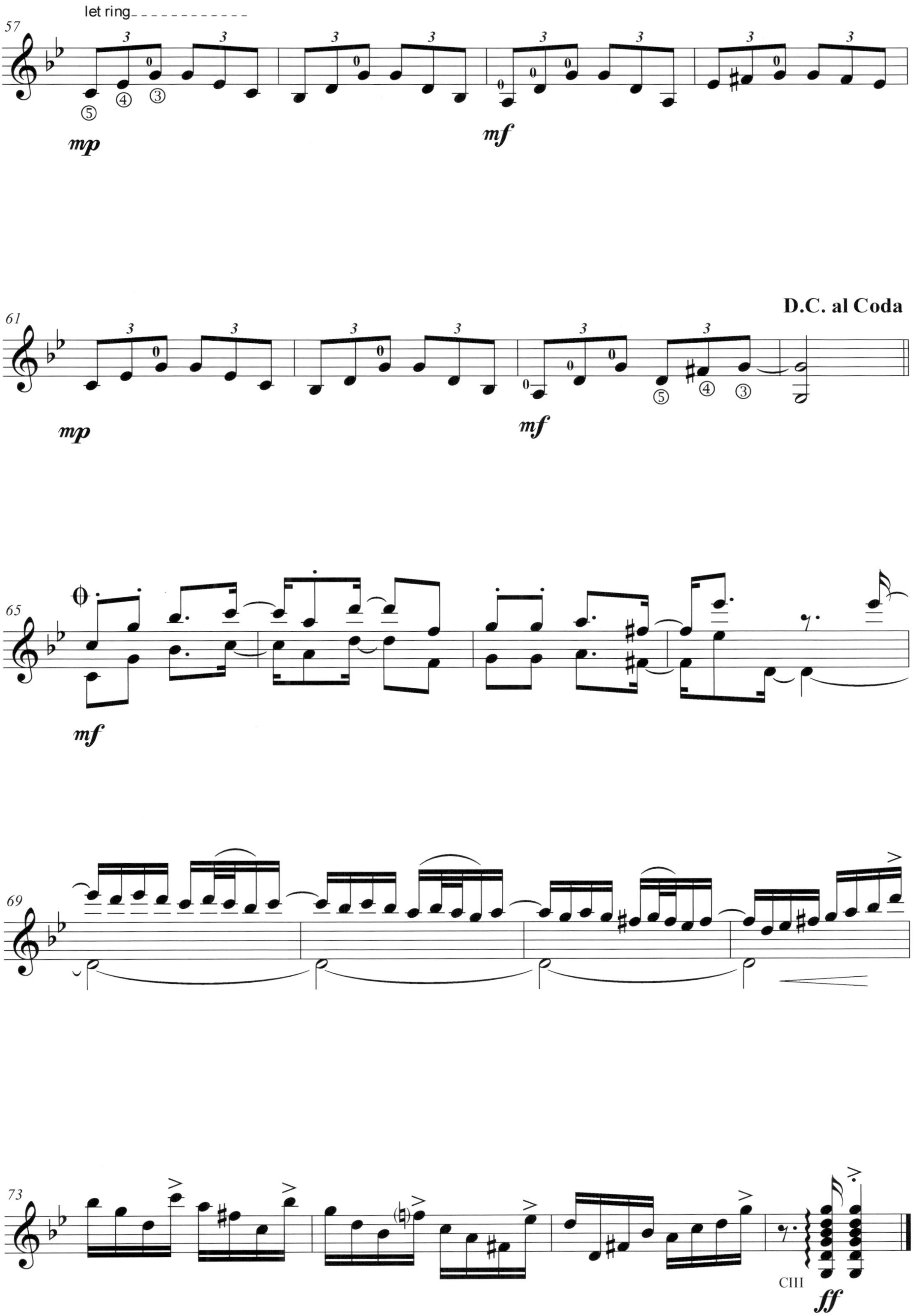
let ring
mp
mf
D.C. al Coda
CIII
ff

About the Author

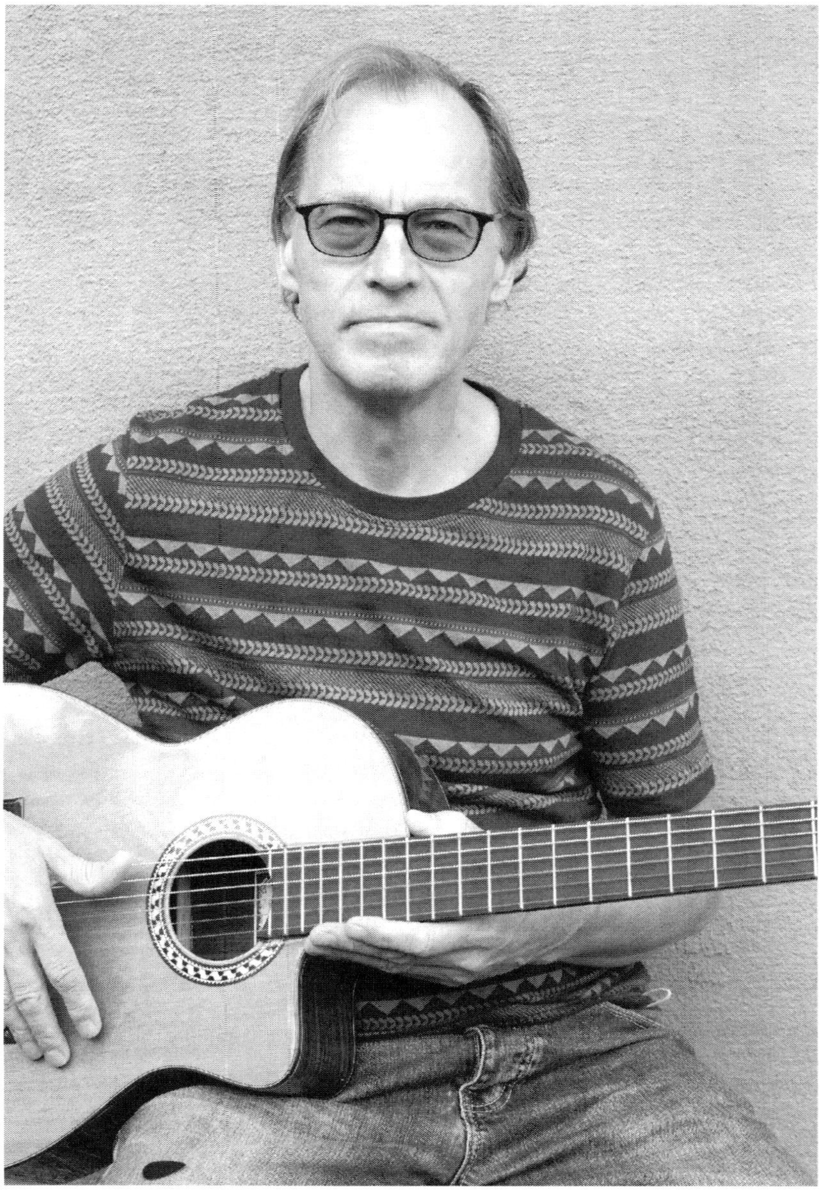

Photo by Okko Pennanen

Keijo Pennanen

Keijo Pennanen's musical journey began with the classical themes and hymns he was exposed to in grade school in Finland. As a young rock music fan, he learned to play drums and guitar. Playing the guitar, songwriting and performing with a pop band were the primary musical activities of his teen years.

In his twenties, having developed an interest in jazz, Pennanen enrolled at Berklee College of Music in Boston, Massachusetts. Berklee provided an invaluable learning experience in harmony, composition, arranging, solo guitar performance, and ensemble playing. He graduated from Berklee in 1986, with honors.

Pennanen has worked as a guitar and ensemble teacher at The Pop & Jazz Conservatory in Helsinki, Finland since 1988. Besides teaching, he has been an active composer and performer, mainly with his own groups. To date, he has released two CDs of original music. Other published works include the guitar lessons he penned for *Guitar Player Magazine* in the late 90's and early 2000s.

Today, Pennanen finds inspiration in classical music and specializes in composing solo guitar pieces for plectrum guitar. *Contemporary Picking Etudes for Guitar* (30620M) and *Achieving Guitar Artistry: Lyrical Etudes* (30698M), published by Mel Bay Publications, Inc. in 2017 and 2019 respectively, are the direct result of these influences and efforts.